RESTITUTION

BOOKS BY PAUL BRODEUR

Fiction
The Sick Fox
The Stunt Man
Downstream

Nonfiction
Asbestos and Enzymes
Expendable Americans
The Zapping of America
Restitution
Outrageous Misconduct

18 95
80u

RESTITUTION

*The Land Claims of the Mashpee,
Passamaquoddy, and Penobscot
Indians of New England*

by Paul Brodeur

Afterword by Thomas N. Tureen

Northeastern University Press

BOSTON

Designed by Richard C. Bartlett

Most of this book appeared originally as articles in *The New Yorker*, in slightly different form.

Library of Congress Cataloging in Publication Data

Brodeur, Paul.
    Restitution, the land claims of Mashpee, Passamaquoddy, and Penobscot Indians of New England.
        1. Mashpee Indians—Claims. 2. Mashpee Indians—Land tenure. 3. Passamaquoddy Indians—Claims.
Passamaquoddy Indians—Land tenure. 5. Penobscot
Indians—Claims. 6. Penobscot Indians—Land tenure.
7. Indians of North America—New England—Claims.
I. Title.
KF8208.B76   1985   346.7304'3'08997   84-29635
                    347.3064308997
ISBN 0-930350-69-3 (alk. paper)

Composed in Caledonia by Crane Typesetting Service, Barnstable, Massachusetts. Printed and bound by The Murray Printing Company, Westford, Massachusetts. The paper is Glatfelter Offset, an acid-free sheet.

Manufactured in the United States of America
90 89 88 87 86 85   5 4 3 2 1

For Mother, David, and Valjeanne,
and to Vernon Smith,
who first told me about the Mashpees

Contents

Illustrations

PART ONE

The Mashpees

The Mashpees

In the autumn of 1977, a trial took place in federal district court in Boston to determine whether the several hundred Wampanoag Indians who live in the town of Mashpee, on Cape Cod, are a legally constituted tribe. It was a landmark case, to say the least, for not only did the question of tribal definition go to a jury for the first time in the United States but hinging on the outcome was the right of the Mashpees, as they have long been called, to a second trial, which would determine the validity of their claim to eleven thousand-odd acres of undeveloped land—approximately three-quarters of the town—whose worth had been estimated at fifty million dollars. In a suit filed in August of 1976, the Mashpees asserted that the land had been taken from them illegally by a process that began in 1842, when the Commonwealth of Massachusetts divided ancestral lands that had been held in common by the Indians and parceled them out to the Mashpees individually, and that culminated in 1870, when the legislature adopted laws changing the old Mashpee Indian District into an ordinary town and conveying the remaining tribal lands to the town. By doing so, according to the plaintiffs, the legislature had violated the federal Nonintercourse Act of 1790, which was passed by the First Congress to protect the Indians from land grabbers, and which has been amended, but preserved, by subsequent Congresses to the present time. The Nonintercourse Act prohibits the sale of Indian lands without the express approval of Congress, and it does so in very specific terms. It states that "no sale of lands made by any Indians, or any nation or tribe of Indians within the United States, shall be valid to any person or persons, or to any state, whether having the right of preëmption to such lands or not, unless the same shall be made and duly executed at some public treaty held under the authority of the United States."

Shortly after its passage by the First Congress, the act was explained to members of the Seneca Nation in New York by President

George Washington, who told them that "when you find it in your interest to sell any part of your lands, the United States must be present, by their agent, and will be your security that you shall not be defrauded in the bargain you make." Washington went on to assure the Senecas that the act was designed to demonstrate "the fatherly care the United States intends to take of the Indians." During the century that followed, the first President's paternal feelings for the Indians occupied precious little space in the hearts of most of his countrymen. Territory west of the Mississippi was expropriated by a succession of Congresses, whose members simply stole Indian land "fair and square" by ratifying a series of treaties and approving virtually every land-taking proposal that came before them. In regard to the eastern part of the country, the Nonintercourse Act was virtually ignored, apparently on the convenient assumption (Washington's words to the Senecas notwithstanding) that its provisions applied only to federally recognized tribes out West. This assumption had now come back to haunt the owners of former Indian tribal land in the East, for recent court decisions had determined that the provisions of the Nonintercourse Act applied to all Indian tribes, whether they were federally recognized or not, and to tribes within the states that evolved from the thirteen original colonies as well as those in other parts of the country. As a result, whereas Western tribes had little legal recourse except to complain to the Indian Claims Commission that they were improperly compensated for their tribal lands, Eastern Indians from Maine to Louisiana began laying direct claim to the land itself on the ground that it had been taken from them in violation of the law.

The amount of real estate at stake was significant by any standard. In Maine, members of the Passamaquoddy Tribe and the Penobscot Nation were claiming twelve and a half million acres—more than half the state. They had already won a decision in the federal Court of Appeals for the First Circuit affirming that they came under the federal protection afforded by the 1790 statute, and they were in the process of negotiating a settlement. In Massachusetts, not only were the Mashpees putting forward their claim but the Wampanoag Indians of Gay Head, on Martha's Vineyard, were seeking the return of two hundred and thirty-eight acres, and their potential claim could include the entire twenty-five hundred acres of the town. In Rhode Island, the Narragansett Indians, who had filed suit in 1975 for thirty-two hundred acres in Charlestown—a town on Block Island Sound—had agreed to a settlement of nineteen hundred acres. In Connecticut, the Western Pequots, the Schaghticokes, and the Mohegans were suing for a total of nearly four thousand acres, and had already won two court decisions holding that the passage of time could not bar their claims under the provisions of the Nonintercourse Act. In New York, the Oneidas had laid claim to two hundred and forty-six thousand acres bordering the lake that bears their name. After winning a unanimous Supreme Court decision allowing them to bring suit in federal court, the Oneidas had subsequently won a decision from the federal district court on remand, holding that they were, indeed, entitled to recovery. Elsewhere in New York, the Cayugas were seeking sixty-four thousand acres, including a three-mile-wide strip around the northern half of the lake named after them; and the St. Regis Mohawks were demanding the return of fifteen thousand acres near the St. Lawrence River. All three claims were being supported by the Department of Justice and the Department of the Interior, whose officials were planning to file additional suits on behalf of the tribes for recovery of the lands and for monetary damages resulting from nearly two centuries of trespass. In South Carolina, the federal government had put together a task force to work on a settlement in the case of the Catawbas, who had laid claim to a hundred and forty-four thousand acres. And in Louisiana the Chitimacha Tribe was seeking the return of some eight hundred acres in the southern part of the state, near the Gulf of Mexico.

Not surprisingly, the sheer size of these claims and the rulings already made in favor of some of the Eastern tribes had produced consternation and debate at virtually every level of government, from the Office of the President on down. The rulings had also called into question the fundamental allegiance of the nation to its judicial system. In Congress, for example, where the possibility that the Eastern Indians might win the return of their tribal lands had been called the controversy of the decade, Representative William Cohen, of Maine, who was considered a liberal for his work in favor of impeachment during the Watergate hearings, had proposed that the claims of the Maine tribes be wiped out and the tribes be permitted to sue only for the value of the land when taken—two centuries ago—plus simple interest.

The impact of the economic problems and the political pressure arising from Indian land claims could be seen in the chain reaction that took place in Mashpee, where, between 1965 and 1975, real-estate development had been by far the largest industry, and where the year-round population had grown from six hundred and sixty-five to nearly twenty-five hundred. After the Indians filed suit, banks refused to grant mortgages and loans, land development halted, construction came to a standstill, and people found it difficult, if not impossible, to sell their homes. This situation produced some overblown and illogical rhetoric. One of the white selectmen in Mashpee warned his fellow-townspeople that "you and I are an endangered species," and that the Indian-rights movement was a cancer that could "destroy the United States of America as we know it now and as it was conceived by our Founding Fathers." Another selectman, who apparently missed the point of the whole case, declared, "We can't be held responsible for what our ancestors did to the Indians more than one hundred years ago."

In this mood, the selectmen rejected all attempts to settle the matter out of court, including a proposal by a special representative of President Carter that a federal mediator be appointed. The case went to trial in a federal court in Boston on October 17, 1977, and on January 4, 1978—after thirty-eight days of testimony and the presentation of thousands of exhibits—it went to an all-white jury of eight men and four women, who were instructed by Judge Walter J. Skinner to determine whether the Mashpees were a legally constituted tribe at certain key dates in their history. Two days later, the jury declared that although the Mashpees were a tribe for an eight-year period between 1834, when the Indian District was created by the legislature, and 1842, when the legislature authorized formal partition of the district land among the Indians, they were not a tribe in 1790, when the Nonintercourse Act was passed by Congress; or in 1869, when the legislature first allowed them to sell their lands to non-Indians; or in 1870, when the legislature abolished the Indian District and incorporated it as a town; or in 1976, when the Mashpees filed their suit. The verdict was a standoff in that neither side was able to claim a clear-cut victory, but the ambiguity of the jury's decision puzzled many people. "We have a mystery," said one of the attorneys who had argued the case for the Indians. "We have a tribe that was in existence in 1834. What became of it?"

On January 26th, both sides submitted arguments—requested by Judge Skinner—as to what action could validly be based on the jury's verdict, lawyers for the Mashpees arguing that it had internal inconsistencies and was illogical, and the defense asking for a judgment of dismissal. On March 24th, Judge Skinner upheld the jury and dismissed the Indians' suit, declaring that the Mashpees had failed to substantiate their assertion of tribal existence, and had proved only that they were an ethnic group "like any other." The dismissal marked the first outright defeat for any of the Eastern tribes in recent years. It was greeted with only cautious optimism by white residents of Mashpee, however, for they did not expect the cloud on land titles to be removed until the appeal process had been exhausted.

For their part, the Mashpees reacted to the verdict and the dismissal with a mixture of disappointment and resignation. To some outside observers, it appeared that the Indians had gambled on the fairness of the American judicial system and lost. One attorney declared that if the case demonstrated anything it was that Indians had better learn not to go before juries. Whether the Mashpees would have fared any better at the hands of Congress or a federally appointed mediator is, however, another matter. Certainly few things that have occurred in the three hundred and fifty-odd years since they first came in contact with whites could have led them to believe so, for during this entire period they have been faced with a seemingly endless series of no-win situations. In short, as anyone who knows the history of the Mashpees can attest, losing is nothing new to them.

I paid my first visit to Mashpee in 1962. It was a midweek afternoon in late September—a day filled with intimations of the season's changing—and I had put a fly rod, a pair of hip boots, and a basket creel in the trunk of my car and driven west across Cape Cod from Orleans to Mashpee to go trout fishing. The distance is about thirty-five miles. Orleans, where I spent my vacations in those days, is on lower Cape Cod, nearly two-thirds of the way to Provincetown, and Mashpee lies on the upper Cape, near the canal. The town of Mashpee, an irregularly shaped tract of land that extends north from Nantucket Sound nine miles into the interior of the peninsula, is bounded on the west by Falmouth, on the north by Sandwich, and on the east by Barnstable, and it was a place I had been intending to visit for some time, not only because I kept hearing that the trout fishing was excellent, but also because of its history. Mashpee, I had been told, had the distinction of being the only town on Cape Cod that was not settled by Englishmen. It was settled by Wampanoag and Nauset Indians. The fact is that Mashpee was never really settled

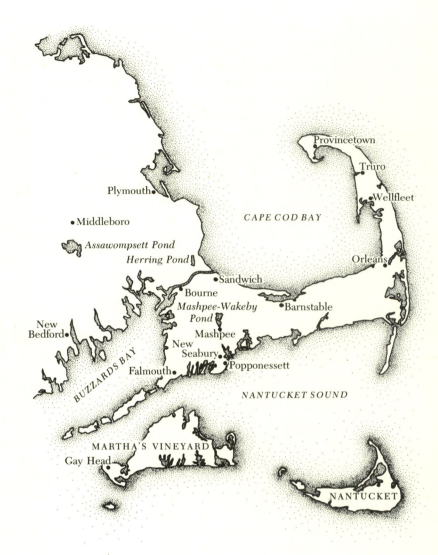

Map of Cape Cod, showing Mashpee.

in any formal sense of the word. It was simply inhabited by the Wampanoags and their Nauset relatives, whose ancestors had been coming there to fish for herring and to gather clams and oysters since the earliest aboriginal times, and whose local descendants currently represent, with the exception of the Penobscots and the Passamaquoddies of Maine, the largest body of Indians in New England. Mashpee was also said to be unusual in another respect. To a remarkable degree, I was given to understand, the six hundred and fifty year-round residents of the town had survived as a race of Indians, notwithstanding a history involving English settlers, African slaves, Hessian mercenaries, Portuguese Negroes from the Cape Verde Islands, and black American veterans of the Second World War—all in all, a mixture that, one might suppose, could easily have obliterated the original strain.

The village of Mashpee lies in the northern section of the town, at the south end of Mashpee-Wakeby Pond, and is linked by several narrow, winding roads with Route 28, which parallels the shoreline of Nantucket Sound. On the day of my first visit there, I turned off onto one of these roads and drove past fifteen or twenty frame houses. Some of them were painted and others were covered with weathered cedar shingles, and most of them looked as if their occupants lived in them all year and didn't have much money; several of the back yards contained such residual clues to poverty as rusted kerosene drums, discarded refrigerators, and the stripped remains of old cars. After a mile or so, I came to a small wooden building identified by a sign: "Mashpee Post Office." Beyond, the road climbed a slight rise, and I emerged into an open area shaded by some tall elm trees, where another road entered from the left. Here, facing the junction, stood a store with a sign that read "Ockry Trading Post." A fire station with a sagging roof and walls that were covered with curling shingles stood beside the store. I took the road to the left and drove up a hill past a modern brick school and a shack identified by a sign as the "Mashpee Library." Diagonally across the road was a Baptist church of uncertain age and style, with shingles stained a dark, glowering brown. That seemed to be the end of the settlement, so I drove back to the junction, pulled up before the Ockry Trading Post, and got out. Overhead, a few leaves were drifting off the elms, and some gulls were soaring inland on a stiff southwesterly breeze. A pair of hounds lay snoozing by the wall of the ramshackle fire station. Except for the gulls and the hounds, there wasn't a sign of life.

I went into the trading post and found it to all appearances equally deserted. It was one of those small, dingy country stores which seem to be stocked with a little of everything. What had not been stuffed into cases and racks, or piled on shelves and counters, hung from hooks fastened to the walls and to wooden posts that supported the ceiling. I took a few steps along a cluttered aisle leading to the rear, and then turned and started back toward the front. I was about to call out when I was stopped short by the sight of a large mounted trout hanging above the entrance. It was a brook trout about twenty-four inches long, and it was a beauty. While I was admiring it, a woman stepped out from the shadows behind a counter to my left. She was a thin, pale-complexioned woman in her late thirties, with long black hair and large brown eyes, and as I turned toward her, startled, she smiled shyly and asked if she could help.

"Can you tell me where that trout was caught?" I said, pointing to the fish above the doorway.

"I'm afraid I can't," she replied. "My father-in-law, Ferdinand Mills, caught it many years ago, but I don't know whether it came from Mashpee Pond or from one of the streams. If my husband, Elwood, were here, he could probably tell you, because he's a fanatic about fishing and knows all the best places to go. I take it you're a fisherman, too."

I said I was, and introduced myself, explaining that I had come to Mashpee not only to fish but in the hope of learning something about the town and its inhabitants.

At this, Mrs. Mills shook her head. "I can't help you there, either," she said. "You see, I'm not a native. I'm of Italian descent, and I was born and raised in Philadelphia. If you're interested, though, I guess the best person to see around here would be Mabel Avant. She's supposed to know more about the town than anyone else. You should also talk with my husband's younger brother, Earl. He lives in Falmouth, where he's director of athletics at the high school. Earl is chief of the Mashpee Wampanoag Tribe here and president of a local group that's been raising funds to restore the old Indian meetinghouse."

The front door banged open just then as two small boys burst in and went directly to a glass case filled with candy. One of them had copper-colored skin and the angular facial features of an Indian; the other was darker, with softer features, suggesting black ancestry. The boys had only a few pennies to spend, and Mrs. Mills, who greeted

them by their first names, waited patiently while they decided what
to buy. At last, having completed the transaction, they darted out,
and she looked fondly after them as they ran across the road. Turning
back to me, she said, "I suppose it might surprise you—it surprises
some strangers, at least—to know that those two youngsters are brothers. There has been mixed ancestry in Mashpee for many generations,
but it's something people here don't talk about much. As for the
meetinghouse, it's a sort of rallying point for the people of Mashpee,
and if you have time to spare you ought to visit it. It's the oldest
church on Cape Cod, and it's the oldest Indian church in the United
States. To get there, you just follow Meetinghouse Road, which is the
first left beyond the school."

I thanked Mrs. Mills, went out and started my car, and, having
decided to save the fishing for another day, took the road to the
meetinghouse. For a couple of miles, I drove through the kind of
jungle that covers much of the interior of Cape Cod—a tenacious,
thirsty-looking, and nearly impenetrable tangle of cedars, pitch pine,
scrub oak, wild grapevines, and blueberry bushes, with here and there
the charred trunk of some larger tree, ravaged by a forest fire. Then,
abruptly, I came upon the meetinghouse—small, square, with cedar-
shingled sides and a clapboard front—standing alone in a clearing at
one side of the road. It was hemmed in on three sides by tombstones
of a burial ground and, beyond them, the bleak woods, and it had a
chaste, Spartan symmetry well suited to its austere background. Un-
like many other old New England meetinghouses, it had survived
through the years without the embellishment of a steeple or a belfry
atop its peaked roof. I got out and, after learning from the inscription
on a bronze tablet affixed to a nearby rock that the meetinghouse was
built in 1684 and moved to its present site some three decades later,
I walked around the building to examine it in greater detail. Grooved
pilasters stood at either end of the façade, topped by frieze boards
and cornices, and in the center was a large and typically Colonial door,
flanked by narrow, vertical windows and by pilasters of its own, and
topped by a molded lintel. Above the door were two oblong windows,
and high up in the center of the façade was a fifth window, small and
triangular, whose two upper sides paralleled the pitch of the roof. In
each side of the building was set a pair of large shuttered windows,
each with twenty-four panes of glass, and in the rear was a semicircular
pulpit window.

For the next half hour, I wandered through the burial ground,

The old Indian meetinghouse. Photograph by Carol Robinson.

reading inscriptions on the tombstones. Many of the names were Indian (Pocknett, Attaquin, Webquish, Keeter, Queppish, and Couett, for example); others were English (Amos, Cobb, Peters, and Stevens), adopted by the Mashpees from the settlers; and a few were derived from the Portuguese-African immigrants who came to Massachusetts from the Cape Verde Islands around the beginning of the century. The tombstones were mostly of slate, which in some instances had so weathered and flaked away that the inscriptions were barely legible. The oldest grave I came across belonged to Deacon Zacheus Pop-munnet, who died on October 2, 1770, at the age of fifty-one. Not far from it was a stone marking the grave of Ebenezer, son of Nancy Squib, who died at sea on October 23, 1849, "aged 17 y'rs 2 mo's." Part of the burial ground borders on busy Route 28, and not until I reached it and saw cars speeding by with their headlights on did I realize that night was approaching. By the time I got back to the meetinghouse, the woods at the edge of the clearing were dark, the gray stones of the burial ground had merged with the rough turf around them, and only the sky and the silvery cedar sides of the old church retained the last light of day.

On my way home, I stopped at a filling station and called Earl Mills at his house in Falmouth. I told him of my visit to Mashpee that afternoon and asked if I could come over sometime and talk to him about the town. "I don't see why not," he replied. "How about toward the end of the week—say, Friday afternoon?" I said Friday would be fine, and we agreed to meet around four o'clock at the high-school football field, where he would be coaching the freshman team. He recommended that I also talk with Mabel Avant, and I said that I was already planning to. "Mabel's our unofficial historian," he went on. "She's an elderly lady and not always very kindly toward strangers to begin with, but I'll give her a ring and tell her you're coming. She has always been interested in preserving our heritage, and she'd been urging us to restore the meetinghouse for years before we finally got around to it, back in 1956. By that time, the place was a terrible mess. We've already spent nearly ten thousand dollars on it, and we're going to need about fifteen thousand more. Some of this will come from admission fees to our annual powwows, and we're hoping that the rest will be made up by public donations. Raising funds has been a terrific effort, but it's been worthwhile. That old church means more to us than anyone can know."

The meetinghouse was built for the Indians near the shore of Santuit Pond, in 1684, by Shearjashub Bourne, of Sandwich. Bourne wanted some land near the Mashpee River as the site for a gristmill, and the Indians, who had become Christians, and who up until that time had met for worship beneath an oak tree, wanted a permanent church. It was one of the few decent bargains they ever managed to strike with the white man. Shearjashub Bourne, however, had come well recommended. His father, Richard Bourne, an agent for Plymouth Colony and the town of Sandwich, had been the Indians' trusted friend for years. In fact, Richard had been preaching to the Mashpees—they were commonly called the South Sea Indians in those days, because they lived near Nantucket Sound, which the Dutch had named the South Sea—since 1657. He had also looked after their temporal interests by arranging for them to obtain a written deed for the land they lived on—some eighteen thousand acres—from a pair of local sachems named Weepquish and Tookenchosun. This deed was executed on December 11, 1665, and in it the two chieftains declared that "wee freely give these lands forementioned unto the South Sea Indians and their Children forever, and not to bee sold or given away from them by anyone without all their Consents thereunto."

Thanks to the elder Bourne's beneficent guardianship and the relative isolation of Cape Cod, the inhabitants of Mashpee, who around that time also became known as Praying Indians, were not involved in the Indian uprising called King Philip's War, which broke out in 1675, and thus they escaped the savage reprisals of the victorious whites, who elsewhere in New England used the rebellion as a pretext for slaughtering the Indians and appropriating their land. (By the time the war ended, in 1676, at least half of the two thousand members of the Wampanoag Nation had either been killed or captured and sold into slavery, and in the following years Mashpee became a refuge for some of the survivors.) In 1685, the year in which Richard Bourne died, the original deed from Weepquish and Tookenchosun to the Mashpees was officially confirmed by the General Court of Plymouth Colony, which granted "said land to the said Indians, to be perpetually to them & their children, as that no part of them shall be granted to or purchased by any English whatsoever, by the Court's allowance, without the consent of all the said Indians."

Six years later, when Plymouth Colony was united with the Massachusetts Bay Colony to form the Massachusetts Colony, two hundred and fourteen adult Indians were living on the Mashpee plantation, as it was called, and they found themselves officially consigned to the protection of the new government. Their spiritual interests were looked after by missionaries who were appointed by the Society for the Propagating of the Gospel Among the Indians in North America, and after 1746 their secular affairs were managed by overseers who were appointed by the General Court.

As early as 1748, the Mashpees were bitterly protesting the actions of the overseers, telling the court that "we are more hurt since they have intermeddled about our lands and meadows," and that "we lived better before they came." By 1760, the situation had become so intolerable that they sent Reuben Cognehew, a Mohegan Indian who was living among them, to England to appeal directly to the new King, George III. Cognehew's journey turned out to be an ordeal. First, he was shanghaied to be sold into slavery by the captain of the ship he embarked upon in Rhode Island; then he was shipwrecked in the West Indies, and rescued by a British naval vessel, only to be impressed into service as a seaman; and finally, having persuaded a British admiral that he was an Indian on his way to conduct important business with the King, he was allowed to proceed to England, where he presented the monarch with a list of grievances concerning the encroachments of the Massachusetts Colony upon the lands and the fishing rights of the Mashpees. As a result, the King ordered the colony to remedy the situation, and in 1763 the colonial legislature passed a law changing the Mashpee plantation into a legal district and giving its Indian proprietors the right to elect their own overseers.

This improvement in the lot of the Mashpees was, however, only temporary. Although they strongly supported the Colonies during the Revolutionary War—at least twenty-six of them enlisted in the First Continental Regiment, and only one of those survived—the Massachusetts legislature disregarded their sacrifice. In 1788, the legislators repealed all former laws regarding the Mashpees, appointed new overseers to rule the plantation, and granted the overseers oppressive powers over the inhabitants, including the right to lease their lands, to sell timber from their forests, and to hire out their children to labor. The Mashpees drew up petitions complaining against these encroachments, but to no avail. In vain, again, in 1811, the Mashpees voiced bitter opposition when Phineas Fish, a young Harvard minister, was appointed their pastor. Six years later, they sent a pitifully worded petition to the legislature "to grant us the unspeakable privilege of choosing our own overseers," and this plea, too, was disregarded. Meanwhile, the Mashpees were well on the way to becoming the mixture of three races that they are today. "The inhabitants of Mashpee are denominated Indians but very few of the pure race are left; there are Negroes, mulattoes, and Germans," the Reverend James Freeman, a white minister, wrote after visiting the plantation early in the nineteenth century. He was right as far as he went. During the preceding century, escaped Negro slaves had been hospitably received in Mashpee, and at the time of the Revolution a number of Hessian prisoners from General Burgoyne's army, sent there to operate a saltworks, had married the widows of the Indians who had died fighting for the Colonists. As a result, some of their names—Hersch and DeGrasse, for instance—still survive among the townspeople. The Reverend Mr. Freeman neglected to mention, however, that on occasion, since the earliest days of the Pilgrims, local settlers of English stock had also married Mashpee women, and had thus pioneered in thinning the ranks of the pure race. The minister went on to describe the Mashpees' meetinghouse as "a cage of unclean birds" and to disparage their community as a place where "hunting, fishing, and fowling, the usual employments of savages, train them up to be insidious." Again, his account was more critical than complete, for it overlooked the fact that many Mashpee men had abandoned these employments to become seamen and whalers—thereby, incidentally, acquiring contact with the outside world that encouraged them when they returned home to intensify the Indians' protest against the missionaries and overseers who were thrust upon them.

Just before sunset on a Saturday in May of 1833, an itinerant preacher named William Apes presented himself at Fish's residence, and was invited by Fish to preach at the meetinghouse on the following morning. It was an invitation that, certainly by no intention of Fish's, marked a turning point in the lives of the Mashpees. Apes is a curious figure, and to this day he remains a hero of almost messianic proportions in Mashpee. In an autobiography, "A Son of the Forest," he wrote that he was born in the woods near Colrain, Massachusetts, on January 31, 1798; that his father was the son of a white man who had married a descendant of King Philip, the son of Massasoit and the chief of the Wampanoags; and that his mother was a full-blooded Pequot. His early life was filled with hardship, and by the time he arrived in Mashpee a long series of humiliations suffered at the hands of white people had given him a fierce pride in his Indian descent and a strong feeling for social injustice. When Apes mounted the meetinghouse pulpit to preach that Sunday morning, he discovered that the congregation consisted almost entirely of whites from neighboring communities, and upon inquiring later among the Indians he was appalled to learn that the Mashpees would not listen to Fish, preferring to worship out-of-doors with a blind Indian preacher named Joseph Amos, who had organized a Baptist church. The Indians presented Apes with a long list of grievances against Fish and their white overseers, and Apes responded by helping them draft two petitions. One petition, in which they protested the presence of Phineas Fish, was sent to Josiah Quincy, president of Harvard College, who was the trustee of a fund that paid the salaries of Mashpee ministers. The other went to the governor of Massachusetts. It declared that "we, as a tribe, will rule ourselves, and have the right to do so, for all men are born free and equal, says the Constitution of the country," and that "we will not permit any white man to come upon our plantation to cut or carry off wood, or hay, or any other article without our permission, after the 1st of July next." Both Quincy and the governor ignored the petitions, but the challenge implicit in the second was accepted on the morning of the day it came due, by four brothers from Sandwich named Sampson, who drove teams and wagons into the Mashpee woods and began to load timber. Called to the scene by some of the Mashpees, Apes tried to reason with the Sampsons; then, when they persisted, he ordered the Indians to unload the wagons. There was no violence, but the Sampsons took the matter to the authorities, and Apes was arrested and charged with riot, assault, and trespass. Tried by jury in Barnstable County Court, he was convicted and sentenced to thirty days' imprisonment.

That was by no means the end of the matter, however; instead, the "riot" at Mashpee became a cause célèbre in the Commonwealth of Massachusetts, owing largely to the efforts of Benjamin Franklin Hallett, the editor of the Boston *Advocate*, who published a series of editorials championing the Indians' cause. Hallett, who was a native of Osterville, a few miles from Mashpee, had a considerable reputation as a reformer, and after Apes' trial he not only offered his services as counsel to the Mashpees but, when they drew up another petition, printed it in his newspaper. The petition bore the signatures or marks of two hundred and eighty-seven Indians, and asked that they be granted the privilege of managing their own property, of establishing their own municipal regulations, and of electing their own magistrates. When the General Court convened in February of 1834 to hear it, Hallett was on hand to present the Indians' case. He argued that to justify the placing of property and person under guardianship the person must be judged incapacitated as an individual, and that it was false reasoning to take for granted that the Mashpees were incapable of self-government, since they had never had a fair opportunity to test their capacity. He concluded with an appeal that had been composed by the Indians themselves: "Give us a chance for our lives in acting for ourselves. O white man! white man! the blood of our fathers, spilt in the Revolutionary War, cries from the ground of our native soil to break the chains of oppression and let our children go free."

Hallett's performance had its effect on the lawmakers, who passed an act partly restoring the right of self-government to the Indians. Under its terms, Mashpee was again incorporated into a district, and the inhabitants were authorized to choose their own officials and to manage their own affairs, with the assistance of a fiscal commissioner appointed by the Commonwealth. Harvard's President Quincy, however, continued to ignore the petition against Fish, who still controlled the meetinghouse, keeping it under lock and key. Patient as ever, the Indians waited three more years before applying to the General Court for permission to organize a parish of their own, with the right to worship unmolested in their own meetinghouse, and at last, after waiting almost as long again, they were granted this small boon. On July 10, 1840, they convened in the meetinghouse for the first time as an independent congregation, but the indefatigable Reverend Mr. Fish turned up, too, and challenged their decision to put a new lock on the building in token of their having taken possession of it. At this, the patience of the Mashpees finally gave out, and they seized the minister and threw him bodily from the church—an act that marked the end of the white man's meddling with their religious life.

For the next thirty years, the central issue in Mashpee was land, as the Indians were gradually given full control of it. The first step in this direction came in 1842, when the legislature passed a law authorizing the division and distribution of their land in such a way that each Mashpee—man, woman, or child—received sixty acres. Since the Indians were not allowed to sell their land except to each other, however, the new law proved to be detrimental, for by dividing up the common lands of the Mashpees it deprived the district of the woodlots that were its major source of public revenue. The law also empowered the Indians to levy taxes on the land, but, since it further stipulated that their holdings were not to be taken for nonpayment, few of them bothered to pay the levies. As a result, the community operated in the red from the beginning, and the condition of the Mashpees rapidly deteriorated.

In 1859, an investigatory commission appointed by the governor found that the death rate among the persons of Indian descent living in the Mashpee District—there were four hundred and three of them at the time—was alarmingly high, and was attributable principally to disease and suffering caused by extreme poverty and to a widespread habit of intemperance. (By now the population of Mashpee had been augmented by Wampanoags who had been living in small bands at Assawompsett Pond, a few miles south of Middleboro, and at Herring Pond, a dozen miles south of Plymouth, where a missionary reservation had been established in 1655.) As for the Indians' special status and the ancient prohibition against the selling of their lands to outsiders, the commission described the curiously ambivalent position in which the Mashpees found themselves on this issue, stating that they had "so long been subject to the encroachments, exactions, and sharp dealings of the shrewder and more practised men by whom they are surrounded that they have come to look upon the laws which place them in this position as their only safeguard from entire ruin." In the end, the commission recommended that the governor continue to deny the Mashpees the rights of full citizenship (including the right to sell their property to non-Indians), warning that they were not yet ready to manage their affairs prudently.

Ten years later, another committee appointed by the governor saw the problem in a different light. "No Indian, if he wants to seek his fortune elsewhere, can sell his land except to his brethren, who, by the operation of the same proscription which drives him away, are too poor to buy," it reported. "Thus the enterprise which is pushing the outside world ahead is shut out from the Indian 'plantation,' and thus the Indians are shut in to comparative thriftlessness and decay." This assessment of the situation prevailed in spite of the fact that at a formal meeting between the committee and the people of the district the Mashpees voted twenty-six to fourteen against a proposal to permit them to sell their lands to outsiders, and split eighteen to eighteen on the issue of whether they should become citizens. A few months later, the legislature—influenced, no doubt, by the Civil War and

the Emancipation Proclamation, as well as by the desire of the surrounding whites to open up Indian lands for purchase—wiped out all
distinctions of race affecting Indians and persons of Indian blood in
Massachusetts, declaring them to be full-fledged citizens with the right
to take, hold, and convey land and real estate. Then, in 1870, it
directed that Mashpee be incorporated as a town.

During the two centuries since the General Court of Plymouth
Colony had confirmed the deed that granted the land to the Indians
and their children forever, the Mashpees had, of course, undergone
profound changes. They had, in fact, become a brand-new people—
almost, in their way, like the present-day Hawaiians. Some of them
looked as Indian as the head on a buffalo nickel; others had essentially
Negro features; still others could, and occasionally did, pass for white;
and many of them bore a conglomerate resemblance to all three races.
During those centuries, too, they had died in the white man's wars,
they had contracted his addiction to alcohol, and they had been ravaged by his diseases. Moreover, aside from a not always congenial
exposure to his religion, they had enjoyed none of the more positive
advantages of his civilization; for example, sporadic proposals to establish permanent schools for them had come to nothing, and con-
sequently only a few of them could read or write. Now, having been
granted full independence, they were officially, for better or worse,
on their own.

In some ways, independence had proved to be definitely for the
worse—as I began to grasp when, on the afternoon following my first
visit to the town, I went to see Mabel Avant who was living in a small
house that had been built in 1793 by a grandson of Richard Bourne.
The house was about a quarter of a mile west of the Ockry Trading
Post, and was diagonally across the road from the Mill Pond and a
concrete-lined herring run. It was a miserable day, with a cold rain
driven by powerful northeast gusts, and on arriving I made a quick
dash from my car across a spongy lawn to reach her door. After I had
rapped a couple of times, it was opened by a tall elderly woman with
light skin and white hair, who was wearing an ankle-length gingham
dress and moccasins. She had a stern mouth and eyes that were dark
and sad, and she studied me suspiciously and in silence.

"Mrs. Avant?" I said.

"Yes, that's me," she answered sharply. "Well, don't stand there,
come in. Come in out of the rain before you catch your death of cold."

Mabel Avant, Mashpee Wampanoag historian, about 1960.

Stepping inside and closing the door behind me, I found myself in a kitchen that contained an old-fashioned cast-iron range, a sink with a wood-handled pump, and a table and several chairs. At Mrs. Avant's bidding, I hung my coat on a peg beside the door and took a chair at the table, whereupon she sat down opposite me.

"Earl Mills phoned up and told me you'd be coming by to talk about Mashpee," she said. "The trouble is, talking about Mashpee tends to make me feel sad, and, what with the gloomy weather and all, I don't know if I'm in the mood."

I said that I had already read about the long struggle of the Mashpees to achieve independence, but she dismissed that part of the story with a bitter smile and an impatient shake of her head.

"What we Indians had to go through during those first two centuries was terrible, all right, but that's not the saddest part," she said. "The saddest and most ironical part is what happened to us after we got our civil rights and became a town. Few of the heirs of the proprietors who got sixty-acre lots back in 1842 bothered to divide the land they inherited among themselves, you see, or to register individual titles with the land court. Most of them just kept on using the land in the same old communal way we Indians always did for centuries before the white man came over here with his walls and fences and bits of paper. So then, after we were given the right to sell our land, a lot of smart Boston real-estate men came down here to look things over, and in no time at all they had figured out how to cheat us. They would get hold of one of the heirs—usually the poorest, or the most ignorant, or the biggest drinker—and they would buy up his shares for a few dollars or a bottle of liquor. Afterward, they would straightaway to the land court up in Boston and petition for title to the choicest part of the whole parcel. Under the law, the court would then send notices to the heirs whose land abutted the part selected by the petitioner, telling them to appear for a hearing on a certain day. Like as not, though, the heirs couldn't make out the fancy legal talk in those notices, or they were afraid they'd done something wrong, or they were just too plain scared or poor to leave town and go all the way up to the city. Anyway, if those heirs didn't show up for the hearing, the case was forfeited automatically, and the petitioners got the part they wanted. Another way we lost a lot of good land arose during the twenties, when many Mashpee people were so bone-poor that they just skipped paying their taxes, and, on top of that, some of our elected officials—our own people—misused their trust by selling town lands for personal gain. As a result, the town went bankrupt in 1931, and when the state stepped in to help us straighten out our affairs we were forced to sell off even more of our wonderful lands and forests, to pay our debts. Today, most of our lakefront property is owned by outsiders, and the shorefront down in south Mashpee has been made into housing developments. Why, Mashpee is the only town on the whole of Cape Cod that doesn't have a public sea beach for its own residents! I guess a lot of people think it's funny how easy to fool we Indians have been about all this, but I can tell you that it's not funny to us. In fact, it eats at our hearts."

Mrs. Avant frowned at the noise of a shutter banging in the wind, but, when she continued, it was in a more cheerful vein. "There *was* one funny thing, though," she said. "It happened forty years ago, when a wealthy Boston lawyer and some friends got together and arranged with the town selectmen to rent the fishing rights to the Mashpee River. I owned a small piece of land along the river, and pretty soon I discovered that those fishermen were storing their canoes in an old bog house that stood on my property. Now, I had little use for the bog house, but that wasn't the point, and I wrote that lawyer a letter telling him that the days of the white man taking what he wanted from us were over, and ordering him to get his boats out of my bog house. He paid no attention to that letter, so I wrote him another, warning him that I was going to put geese in a dammed-up part of the river that abutted my land. Well, since there's nothing that will gobble up small fish faster than a hungry goose, and since the lawyer had just got through stocking the river with fingerling trout, he decided he'd better do something about it. He came down from Boston to see me, and he ended up buying the land at my price— three times what he offered at first. Even so, we parted good friends, and for years after that he always stopped by to say hello when he came down here to fish."

Mrs. Avant fell silent and gazed reflectively out the window. "As a matter of fact," she said, at last, "sportsmen have been coming to Mashpee for the trout fishing since long before I was born. Daniel Webster was one of the first ones. He started fishing here around 1820, and he kept coming back for the rest of his life. Toward the end of the century, President Grover Cleveland used to come down from his summer place up on Buzzards Bay and fish here with the actor Joseph Jefferson. All of them used to stay at the Attaquin Hotel, right next door, which had one big corner room named for Webster and

*Rhoda Attaquin Sturgis, at the age of 97. Photograph by
Frank G. Speck, 1928. Courtesy of the Museum of the American
Indian, Heye Foundation.*

another named for President Cleveland. Now, there was a lovely old
hotel! I'm sorry to say it burned to the ground five or six years ago.
It was built in 1840 by my great-uncle Solomon Attaquin, who was
the wealthiest man in Mashpee and the master of a coasting ship that
traded from Boston to New York and up the Hudson as far as Albany.
He died about the time I was born, in 1892, so I don't remember
him, but I remember his sister very well. Her name was Rhoda Attaquin Sturgis, and her mother was from Herring Pond. She was born
about 1830 and she lived to be ninety-eight. Aunt Rhoda told me a
lot of stories about Mashpee when I was a girl, and she's the reason
I got interested in our history. She was at the meetinghouse the day
they threw out that white preacher Phineas Fish, and though she was
only ten years old when it happened, she said she would never forget
the commotion he made when they dragged him down the aisle. She
even said that the scuffmarks made by his boots stayed on the floor
for years and years!"

Mrs. Avant went to the sink, pumped some water into a kettle,
and put it on the stove, remarking that she was going to boil water
to make Indian dumplings. "Mashpee people have always loved Indian
dumplings," she said as she returned to her chair. "When I was a girl,
we made them with the same raw cornmeal we fed our horses. My
father, Willard Pocknett, used to say that they stuck to the ribs like
nothing else. We Mashpees always ate a lot of wild game, and we still
do—especially rabbit and venison. Believe it or not, skunk was one
of our greatest delicacies. Most people don't realize how good a nice
young skunk can be, because they don't know how to prepare it. The
trick, of course, is in removing the scent glands, but that's an old
Indian secret. Once that's been done, you parboil the skunk in salt
water and then you bake it in the oven. Skunk has a nice layer of fat,
and it gets beautifully brown, just like a roast of pork. We used to
serve it with cranberry sauce, diced pumpkin, and brown bread. White
people have an idea that cranberries go best with turkey, but, let me
tell you, cranberries were made to go with roast skunk. My goodness,
how I wish the men would bring home skunk the way they used to!
Like a lot of other things in Mashpee, though, skunk seems to have
gone out of style."

The rain had stopped, but the sky was still gray and glowering
when I drove over to Falmouth to keep my Friday-afternoon appoint-

ment with Earl Mills. In those days, Falmouth was a pleasant and prosperous town of about thirteen thousand, some of whom lived in lovely old houses that had been built by whaling and shipping families in the eighteenth and nineteenth centuries. The high-school football field was not far from the center of town, and when I got there I had no difficulty in spotting Mills, who is a descendant of the Webquish family. A slender, ruggedly handsome man in his middle thirties, with close-cropped black hair, dusky skin, and the bluntly sculptured features one associates with Indian ancestry, he was drilling a group of teen-age boys in the art of ball passing. He guessed who I was, and when the practice session broke up he came over and we shook hands. We walked across the field to a locker house, and after he had changed from football pants and jersey into street clothes we drove to his home—an unpretentious ranch house about half a mile away, where we were greeted by his wife, Shirley, and by their four small children. Mrs. Mills, who was part Navajo, was a tawny, intensely pretty woman with brilliant green eyes and a vivacious smile, and after welcoming us she shepherded the children into the back of the house, leaving her husband and me in a large combination living and dining room, where he motioned me toward an easy chair. Then, while building a fire in the fireplace, he started reminiscing about his boyhood in Mashpee.

"When I was kid, I and the young fellows I ran around with couldn't have cared less about our Indian background," he said. "We never participated in any of the tribal ceremonies, we didn't know how to dance, and we wouldn't have been caught dead in regalia. We thought anyone who made a fuss about our heritage was old-fashioned, and we even used to make fun of the people who did. Well, when I came back from the Army, in 1948, I had a different outlook on such matters. You see, there happened to be two other Indians in my basic training company at Fort Dix. One of them was an Iroquois from upper New York State, and the other was a Chippewa from Montana. I was nineteen years old, away from Mashpee for the first time in my life, and, like most soldiers, I was lonely. Then, one night, the Iroquois fellow got up and did an Indian dance in front of everybody in the barracks. The Chippewa got up and joined him, and when I had to admit I didn't know how, I felt terribly ashamed. During the next two years, I had the recurring feeling of not really knowing who or what I was, and I decided that when I got out of the service I would find out and do something about it. So one of the first things I did after I got back home was go and see Mabel Avant, who I heard was trying to interest the townspeople in restoring the old meetinghouse. When she saw that I really wanted to help out, she told me things about my people and our history that I had had no idea of. She got me so worked up about it all that I went straightaway to my father and asked him to show me how to make Indian baskets. Was he surprised! He had learned basketry as a young man from old Eben Queppish, who was the last master basketmaker in Mashpee. Nobody in Mashpee had made baskets in years, and my father was very pleased to find that I wanted to keep the art alive. What with soaking and stripping maplewood and weaving the bark into baskets, we both kept busy for several months."

Mills sat down, threw a leg over the arm of his chair, and switched to another subject that was a source of pride to him—the Mashpee baseball team, which had won the semi-professional championship of Cape Cod in the summer of 1948. "All of us who played on it that summer were of Indian descent," he said. "I was at shortstop, and one of the outfielders was my brother Elwood. He's a born athlete— so good that when he played football for Falmouth High, before the war, the Boston newspapers called him the Jim Thorpe of Cape Cod. Donald Hicks was our right-handed pitcher. His father, who played in the thirties, was the greatest pitcher in Mashpee history. He and my mother's brother George Oakley, who caught him, made quite a battery. My Uncle George was a slugger and a clown to boot, and when he came up to bat he used to wave the outfielders farther out and tell them to go peek in his mailbox, which was a quarter of a mile down the road. He had a mouthful of gold teeth and he was always smiling, and, like a lot of the other Indian fellows in town, he was quite a drinker. He always carried a flask of sneaky in his hip pocket, and when he and Jeff Hicks had conferences on the mound you'd sometimes see them taking a slug or two from it. Once, when some Red Sox scouts came down to look them over, Jeff Hicks and Uncle George put on a terrific show. Hicks pitched a two-hitter, and in the ninth inning Uncle George nailed a runner trying to steal second, and at the end of the game they met halfway between the mound and the plate and toasted the crowd."

Mills said that in the autumn following his discharge from the Army he put basketmaking and ballplaying aside temporarily and entered Arnold College, in Milford, Connecticut, where he majored in physical education. "It seemed the sensible thing to do," he went on.

"Sports were always the most important thing to all of us Mashpee boys, and it's easy enough to see why. Coming from a tiny town where for nearly three hundred years our people had been considered—and had considered themselves—different from the people all around them, and where there was no tradition of getting an education, Mashpee boys had no real confidence in themselves once they had to leave our little grade school and go on to Falmouth High. We felt like strangers in another world, and we were desperately afraid we wouldn't be able to make a go of it. But skill at sports was admired in that new world, and we were good at them. They gave us what we needed to stand on our own—some of us, that is. Others couldn't make a go of it anyway. After I graduated from college, I got my job at Falmouth High, and since then I've seen the same thing happen time and again. I watch Mashpee boys and girls getting off the bus at the start of the school year and I know in my heart that they're every bit as shy and afraid as I was the day I first arrived. I know that because of this many of them will drop out after a while and just stay home in Mashpee, where they feel more secure. I keep an eye on them, of course, and I try to encourage them to stick it out, but since the insecurity originates in Mashpee, I suspect that the problem will have to be solved there."

The fire was burning low, and Mills got up and threw a fresh log on it; then, standing with his back to the hearth and an elbow resting on the mantel, he told me that Mashpee was in a state of unrest, much of it stemming from the Second World War. "Before the war, Mashpee was a clannish little village of about three hundred people—not even half what it is now—where everybody not only knew everybody else but almost everybody was distantly related," he said. "During the war, however, when thousands of soldiers and airmen were stationed nearby at Camp Edwards and Otis Field, trouble broke out between Southern white and Negro troops, and the military authorities persuaded the people in Mashpee to let them build a U.S.O. center for the colored servicemen on their land. The colored fellows were made to feel welcome in Mashpee, and they got to like the town so much that after the war a great many of them came back and settled in it. Unfortunately, this caused a certain amount of resentment on the part of some of the older natives who—though they are, as we all are, of mixed blood—consider themselves Indian and want the town to remain Indian. Another cause of unrest is the housing developments that are being built down in South Mashpee, on Nantucket

Earl Mills, chief of the Mashpee Wampanoag Tribe, sitting by the flume. Photograph by Leslie Friedman.

Sound. Mashpee people are hoping that they'll provide a new source of tax revenue, but they also know that such developments bring in outsiders—who in this case are bound to be mostly, if not entirely, white. For this reason, the Mashpee Indians are afraid of losing political control of the town, and since our whole history has been one long struggle to free ourselves from domination of others, it's a disturbing issue."

Before leaving, I told Mills that I had learned from his sister-in-law that he was chief of the Mashpee Wampanoag Tribe, and that I wondered what responsibilities the job entailed these days.

"It's mostly a matter of raising funds to restore our meeting-house," he said. "And that means planning and running our annual powwows. They're held on the weekend following the Fourth of July. They're the biggest social event of the year in Mashpee, and the admission fees paid by the general public are our biggest source of outside income. The climax of the powwows is an old-fashioned clam-bake, prepared by members of the Mashpee Wampanoag Rod and Gun Club. The Rod and Gun is one of the strongest organizations in town. In fact, the importance of fishing and hunting to Mashpee people can hardly be exaggerated. It's a way of life. During deer season, in December, and when the trout season opens, in the spring, most of the fellows in town don't even bother going to work. My brother Elwood, for example, just closes up the trading post and takes off. He must spend nearly as much time on the water each year as he does on land. Just mention the idea of going fishing to him and then try to keep up with him. Elwood is the most patient fisherman I've ever known, too—except, perhaps, our father, who once spent an entire summer going after a huge trout he discovered in a cranberry-bog sluiceway."

"Is that the one hanging over the door of your brother's store?" I asked.

Mills frowned and shook his head. "I'm not sure," he replied. "I'll have to ask him."

Before leaving, I told Mills that I would like to visit Mashpee again someday, when he would have time to show me around a bit.

"Sure, he said. "almost any weekend. As a matter of fact, I'm going over there tomorrow to look in on a rummage sale we're holding for the benefit of the meetinghouse. Why don't you meet me around noon at my brother's store?"

Next day, the wind was still blowing hard and cold from the northeast, but there were patches of blue sky showing through the clouds. When I arrived at the Ockry Trading Post, shortly after noon, Earl and Elwood Mills were both there. Like Earl, Elwood was soft-spoken and serious, but physically the two brothers had little in common. Elwood was an extremely large, heavyset man in his early forties, with tremendously muscular forearms. His features did not have the blunt Indian quality of Earl's, and he might easily have been mistaken for someone of Italian or Latin descent if it had not been for his eyes, which, like most Indians' eyes, were somber and very black.

After some preliminary small talk, I remarked that I had heard great things about the trout fishing in Mashpee, and at that, Elwood, whose attention had been wandering, looked at me gravely and said that he had been raising some big fish in Mashpee-Wakeby Pond during the past couple of weeks. Then, when I expressed interest, he asked me, in a seemingly offhand manner, if I would like to go out with him for an hour or so. I jumped at the offer, and Earl said he guessed he'd come along, too, but first he wanted to drive over to the rummage sale to sample some of the fish chowder that the women of the community were ladling out as a special attraction. It was then agreed that he would take me with him, and that as soon as Elwood could get someone to mind the store he would pick up his boat and meet us there.

Our destination, about a mile northwest of the store, was the old U.S.O. building—a typical wartime structure, wooden and rambling—which the people of Mashpee used as their town hall. We hadn't been there long—just long enough, in fact, for a bowl of chowder and a cup of coffee and a chat with some of the women in the entrance hall—before Mills' aunt, Mrs. Minnie DeGrasse, poked her head in from the kitchen and said that Elwood was honking for us outside.

"Eat and run," said one of the women we'd been talking to. "That's a Mashpee man for you."

" 'Eat and go fishing' is what you mean," said Mrs. DeGrasse.

Earl and I gulped the rest of our coffee, complimented the women on their chowder, and took our leave. Elwood was waiting for us, parked beside Earl's car in a pickup truck with a twelve-foot aluminum skiff tied in the back, and as soon as he saw us coming he shifted into gear and started off. With Elwood leading the way, we drove northwest a short distance along a paved road and then turned right onto a dirt track that cut through some woods for half a mile and brought us, bouncing over rocks and washouts, to a cove on Mashpee-Wakeby Pond. Elwood parked the truck beside a cottage that had been shuttered up for the season, and Earl and I pulled to a stop alongside, climbed out, and helped him unload the skiff, drag it through a tangle of sumac down to the water's edge, and ease it in, stern first.

At this point, I remembered that I had left my fishing license in my car, which was parked back at Elwood's store. However, when I wondered aloud whether I should return for it, Elwood shook his head. "You don't need a fishing license here," he said quietly. "This is our lake." Returning to the truck, Elwood rigged up an old glass fly rod with a conventional reel, some line that looked considerably the worse for wear, and a nylon leader, to which he tied a white streamer fly. Then we climbed into the skiff, with me in the stern, Elwood in the center seat, and Earl standing in the prow, oar in hand, to push us off.

As soon as we were out on the water, drifting on the momentum of Earl's initial thrust, my companions fell as tensely silent as a pair of sentinels who have heard a noise in the night. Earl crouched in the bow, peering into the water, and Elwood, his head cocked to one side, seemed to be listening for some murmur from the depths of the lake. After a minute or two, Elwood fitted the oars into their locks and, dipping the tips of the blades gently beneath the surface, rowed out toward the middle of the cove. Presently, the bottom disappeared from sight, and Elwood turned toward the southern rim of the cove, where the full force of the wind was driving miniature waves against a steep bank covered with heavy thickets that ended in a tangle of exposed roots at the water's edge. About thirty-five yards offshore, he quietly lowered an anchor into the water and then, while the skiff swung around with the wind, studied the bank intently. Finally, he nodded and turned to me. "Here's where they are," he said, in a near whisper. "The trout come into this cove with the northeast wind to go after minnows that get blown into shallow water. Put the fly as close to the roots as you can, let it sink, and then retrieve it with short, quick jerks, holding the rod tip high."

I stood up and began to cast, but, despite the advantage of having the wind at my back, I found that I could not put the streamer fly closer than ten or fifteen yards to the shore; and since achieving even

that twenty yards or so was more than I was accustomed to, my wrist
and forearm soon began to ache. I kept at it, though, mindful of
Elwood's instructions, as I paused at the end of each presentation to
allow the streamer to sink before jerkily retrieving it to simulate the
erratic movements of an injured minnow. On perhaps my twentieth
retrieve, the line gave an almost imperceptible twitch, and the water
seemed to bulge ever so slightly in the vicinity of the streamer. Taking
this to mean only that the fly had swirled close to the surface, I failed
to give my rod tip the quick upward lift needed to tighten the line
and set the hook, and thus gave the trout—for I realized too late that
there was one—the opportunity to recognize the lure as artificial and
reject it.

Squinting into the glare of the sun that shimmered on the wind-
chopped water, Elwood said simply, "You missed one."

Wanting to rest my wrist for a while, I surrendered the rod to
Elwood, and we changed places in the skiff. He planted his feet apart
in the stern, stripped fifteen or twenty yards of line off the reel, and,
working his forearm like a piston, whipped the rod back and forth
until all the free line was in the air. Then he stripped some more off
the reel, and sent the streamer arching out over the water to settle
lightly within inches of the shore. Nothing came of his first cast, but
on his second, to the base of a giant water-killed oak, he had retrieved
five or six feet of his line when, again, there was that barely discernible
swirl in the water near the streamer. Elwood, reacting even more
swiftly than the trout, gave an upward flick of his wrist to set the hook.
At once, the rod bent like a bow at full draw; then the line sliced
sideways in a great arc through the wavelets, and a moment later a
large trout jumped clear of the surface some thirty yards behind us,
shaking drops of water from the line and leader as it danced for an
instant in the sunlight before it plunged back into the depths.

The trout did not show itself again for several minutes but fought
a deep battle, making half a dozen long lateral runs. It then headed
straight for the skiff, coming so near that, as Elwood hastily took up
slack line, the upper part of his leader emerged from the water and
we could see the trout as a dark shadow about five feet down. Next,
the fish darted to the surface and rolled over on its side, but as Elwood
started to lead it toward the boat it surged away on a powerful run,
taking ten or fifteen yards of line with it. The end was near, though;
after jumping clear of the water again, the trout allowed itself to be
led slowly toward the skiff, and at last Earl was able to reach it with

a broom-handle net and lift it into the boat. It was a brown trout about eighteen inches long—a wonderfully heavy, slab-sided fish with orange spots on a gray belly, and a hooked jaw that pronounced it a male.

Elwood passed the rod back to me and, standing up—my enthusiasm renewed—I tried again. This time, when the telltale swirl came my response was quick enough to set the hook, and I found myself fast to a heavy fish engaging in a series of circular runs, dogging back and forth close to the bottom, and never once breaking water. Tiring eventually, it rose to the surface, where it lay on its side, and Earl scooped it out with the net. This trout was a female—a bit longer than Elwood's, but thinner and not as beautifully marked. Then, just as Elwood stood up and began to cast again, the northeast wind suddenly died away, leaving the surface of the cove calm and placid— no place for trout. Although there were no more strikes, Elwood kept at it until the cove lay in the late-afternoon shadow of the headlands, when even he agreed that it was time to pull up anchor and return to shore.

Elwood beat us back to the trading post, and by the time we arrived he was weighing the trout on his butcher's scale before a gathering of perhaps a dozen townspeople who had come in to do their weekend shopping. Each of the trout weighed slightly more than two and a half pounds, and together they were occasioning admiring comments from the women customers, as well as some searching questions from the men concerning just where they had come from. Smiling courteously at the comments of the women and replying enigmatically to the questions of the men, Elwood wrapped the trout I had caught in a piece of brown paper and held it out to me. I declined it, telling him that I wanted him to have it, but he insisted, saying that he already had his, so I should have mine. I urged him again to keep it, but, patiently and with quiet dignity, he shook his head, and I could see that he was adamant. I turned and asked Earl to accept it, but his response was the same. I had caught it, he said, and therefore it was mine. A hush had fallen over the customers, and, looking around the store, I saw that they were watching me intently with expressions that were neither friendly nor hostile but utterly impassive. I suddenly realized that I had made a mistake, and it occurred to me that I might well be thought presumptuous to propose giving my hosts a trout that

I, as a visitor—an outsider, really—and their guest, had caught in their ancestral waters. Happily, at that moment my eye lit on the mounted trout hanging above the doorway.

"Maybe we could drop it by for your mother and father," I said to Earl. "Do you think they'd like it?"

"I bet they might, at that," Earl replied solemnly.

Elwood, just as solemnly, nodded his approval. Again, he held out the trout to me, and this time I accepted it.

Leaving Elwood to resume his duties as storekeeper, Earl and I drove over to call on his parents, Emma and Ferdinand Mills, who lived in a modest frame house a mile from the trading post, and, entering through the back door, we came on his mother in the kitchen. Smiling with delight, Mrs. Mills, a gracious, white-haired, bespectacled woman in her late sixties, who had served as the town treasurer for thirty-one years, accepted the trout as a present from both of us, put it on a platter, and, bearing it aloft, preceded us into the living room, where her husband, who had served as a selectman in Mashpee for twenty years, was sitting in an armchair reading the paper. "Earl's here with a friend, Grandpa, and look what they brought us," she said. Mr. Mills got to his feet, beaming at Earl and me and then at the fish. He was a stocky, ruddy-faced man, a few years older than his wife, with a merry smile and eyes that reflected more humor than most Indian eyes do, and he shook my hand with an immensely powerful grip and told me I was welcome. Then he examined the trout and said, with an exaggerated sigh, "Ah, you young fellows! You can't imagine what the fishing used to be like around here. Why, when I was a boy, I used to take a knapsack down to the Quashnet River and fill it with native brookies in a couple of hours."

Mrs. Mills returned with the trout to the kitchen, announcing that she was going to cook it for supper, and Earl, his father, and I sat down. I asked Mr. Mills about the fish hanging in the trading post, and he grinned and, closing his eyes and tilting his head back reflectively, said that he had caught it in 1929, in the Quashnet River, and that it had weighed exactly four and three-quarters pounds. "The Quashnet was always my favorite trout stream," he said. "It was one of President Cleveland's favorites, too. In fact, I took that fish out of a deep part of the river known as Cleveland's Hole."

"What about that one in the cranberry sluiceway?" Earl asked.

His father smiled ruefully. "I never did catch that danged trout, Earl," he replied. "I tried hard enough, but as far as I know he died of old age. That was the biggest trout I ever saw, and long after I'd given up trying to get him I used to go down there and lie on my belly on the dam above the sluiceway and just look at him. My guess is he couldn't have weighed less than six or seven pounds."

Before we left, Mr. Mills foraged around in his desk and produced an old tomahawk head, chiselled from a piece of slate-gray stone, smooth and beautifully shaped, with a narrow, tapering base grooved for binding it to a handle with a rawhide thong. Fondling it lovingly, he told me that he had found it on Daniel's Island, in South Mashpee, when he was a boy. "The island was named after Daniel Queppish, who was the grandfather of Eben Queppish, the old basketmaker," he said. "Daniel Queppish's parents had a wigwam and a planting ground there, and, like their forefathers for generations before them, they went to the island in the summertime to be near the oyster beds and the good eel fishing. Well, that was a long time ago, and now Daniel's Island is part of a housing development, but, you know, I have a funny feeling about this tomahawk head. It's something that belonged to my people. It may even have belonged to an ancestor of mine. Why, in some ways it's the most valuable thing I own."

Mr. Mills followed us out into the kitchen, where we said good-bye to his wife—who gave us a peek at the trout, already turning a golden brown in the oven—and then on out to the back yard. For a moment, he stood there looking up at the star-filled night sky, and then he whipped his arm back and forth several times as if he were casting a fly rod. Finally, he extended his hand, grasped mine, and, with his powerful grip, drew me sharply toward him, taking care, however, to keep me on balance by putting his other hand squarely on my shoulder. "Come back and see us sometime," he said slowly. "We'll still be here. There's something that holds us Mashpees to these woods and ponds of ours. We've been here a long, long time, and I expect we're going to be here forever."

In the years that followed, I kept up with events in Mashpee in sporadic fashion. Occasionally, I passed through the town in order to show friends the old meetinghouse—its restoration was completed in 1967—and the Indian graveyard beside it. Once, not long after my initial visit, I paid a call on the developer of a three-thousand-acre vacation and retirement community called New Seabury, which was then being built in South Mashpee, on the shores of Nantucket Sound, where the Indians had always harvested shellfish. The developer was enthusiastic about the prospect of using miles and miles of Mashpee fire roads as bridle paths. Many of them, he explained, had been laid out along old trails that historians call the Indians' "ancient ways." He was contemptuous of the U.S.O. building that served as the town hall, and of the ramshackle fire station, and he made it clear that he hoped to bring Mashpee up a notch or two in the public's estimation. "What's needed in Mashpee is long-range planning," he told me. "We're going to pull what now passes for the center of town down to the traffic circle on Route 28 and we're going to build churches, public buildings, and a shopping area for the entire section of the Cape down there. There'll be parking problems, of course, but we'll handle them with lots of pavement."

When I asked him whether the Indian residents of Mashpee would go along with these plans, he shrugged. "Our ideas reflect what modern Americans are seeking," he replied. "The Mashpees can go along or not. It won't make any difference."

The developer was right, of course. The kind of progress he wanted came to Mashpee, and what the Indians may have wanted made no difference whatever, for they no longer owned the land. Over the next decade, New Seabury spread; the shellfish beds in South Mashpee were largely destroyed; a shopping center was built at the traffic circle on Route 28; land values skyrocketed; and the year-round population of the town of Mashpee increased from six hundred and fifty to more than two thousand. In 1964, a white selectman was elected, and by 1968 the Indians had lost their majority on the board, so they no longer had political control of the town.

The loss of political control and the patronage that went with it came as a tremendous blow to the Mashpees, who had apparently assumed that they would always be able to run the town. The Indians also assumed that even if they did not actually own the land they would always be able to use it as they had in the past. They were taken aback when newcomers who bought homes on the ponds, rivers, and oceanfront in Mashpee posted no-trespassing signs and erected chain-link fences—some even extending out into the water—that prevented the Indians from reaching their traditional fishing places. Since they had always considered the ponds, the rivers, the ocean, and the fish therein a common treasure, it had never occurred to any of them to actually *live* by the water, let alone erect fences in order to prevent common access to it. They were bewildered and depressed by the actions of their new neighbors, and, feeling helpless to do anything about the situation, they grew downcast. For this reason, many observers consider this period to have marked the lowest ebb in their long and troubled history.

Having hit bottom, however, the Mashpees finally realized that if they were to continue as a cultural entity they would have to develop a strategy for survival. The first step was to organize. In 1974, in order to get federal grants that were being made available to Americans of Indian descent, they incorporated the Mashpee Wampanoag Indian Tribal Council, which soon became their legal and business arm in dealing with the local, state, and federal goverments. Early in 1975, the council learned of the key ruling by the United States Court of Appeals for the First Circuit in the dispute between the Passama-quoddy Tribe and the State of Maine: the court had held that the 1790 Nonintercourse Act applied to all Indian tribes, including those that were not federally recognized. The council then got in touch with Thomas Tureen, an attorney for the Native American Rights Fund, (NARF)—a nonprofit law firm, financed by a variety of private foun-dations (primarily the Ford Foundation), that had been formed in 1971 to handle Indian grievances across the nation and was then repre-senting the Passamaquoddies—to find out if the Mashpees might also have a case under the Nonintercourse Act. Tureen, who had been a prime mover in the recent efforts of half a dozen of the Eastern tribes to regain their lands, sent a young lawyer named Barry Margolin to Mashpee in the spring of 1975, and, after listening to the Indians tell how they had lost control of their land, he spent the better part of the next year reconstructing the history of the Mashpees by digging through state, county, and library archives and examining thousands of pages of legislative documents, Colonial records, and land trans-actions. In the spring of 1976, Margolin informed the Tribal Council that the Mashpees did indeed have a case for recovery of sixteen thousand acres of ancestral lands under the Nonintercourse Act, and on August 26th the council filed suit in federal district court against the New Seabury Corporation, the town of Mashpee, and more than a hundred large landholders in the community.

Meanwhile, an ugly incident had taken place, and it united the Mashpees at a crucial time. Earlier in the summer, with the help of federal funds, young people in the town had erected the frames for several wigwams and an Indian longhouse in Attaquin Park, at the south end of Mashpee-Wakeby Pond, and one evening in late July twenty or thirty of them gathered there with a group of visiting Cherokees from Oklahoma to have a clambake and to listen to some Indian drumming and singing. Shortly after midnight, two or three dozen policemen swooped down upon the youths, most of whom were by then asleep. The ranks of police included members of the Mashpee town force and policemen from several surrounding communities, and they were accompanied by dogs. After routing the young people from under their tents and blankets, roughing them up, and confiscating their drums, the police carted twelve of them (including Earl Mills' son, Earl, Jr.) off to jail and charged them with a variety of crimes, such as disturbing the peace, assault, and threatening the lives of officers. Ten months later, in Barnstable County Court, all the youths were acquitted by a judge who declared that they were innocent and should never have been brought before him to begin with. At the time of the arrests, the Mashpees were enraged by the excessive show of force on the part of the police and were convinced that the raid was a naked attempt by the town to intimidate them and put down the Indian movement. A few nights later, some two hundred Indians packed the auditorium in the town hall to vent their displeasure and to demand explanation from the selectmen, who were unable to provide satisfactory answers. As far as the Mashpees were concerned, the incident in Attaquin Park was the last straw. It focussed the anger that had been building in them for years, and it rallied them behind the lawsuit.

Once Mashpee Tribe v. New Seabury Corporation had been filed, relations between Indians and many non-Indians in Mashpee deteriorated rapidly. Appalled by the sudden halt it caused in real-estate sales and the construction of new houses, some whites charged that the Indians were practicing extortion, destroying the basic economy of the town, and causing people to lose their jobs. The Indians pointed out that for years they had endured the highest rate of unemployment on Cape Cod, and that most of them had been forced to make their living outside Mashpee. They also pointed out that land development and housing were a false economic base for the town, in that they would soon come to an end. By October, the town selectmen, who had at first considered the lawsuit something of a joke, had retained James D. St. Clair—the Boston lawyer who defended Richard Nixon in the Watergate-tapes case—at an initial fee of sixty-five thousand dollars. (Eventually, the town's legal fees and disbursements exceeded three hundred thousand dollars.) In their answer to the suit, St. Clair and lawyers for the New Seabury Corporation challenged the plaintiff's assertion that they were a tribe, saying that the Mashpees were a mixed race and could not claim legal status as a tribe. The Mashpees regarded this attempt to disparage their heritage as a tactic of desperation, and declared that they would welcome the opportunity to prove their tribal identity in court. With the battle lines thus drawn, each side set about hiring a team of expert historians and anthropologists and preparing its case.

While this was going on, tension mounted in the town. Anti-white slogans appeared on buildings at the Quashnet Valley Golf Course, in Mashpee, where excavators had unearthed the skeleton of a Wampanoag a year before, and in New Seabury a tennis building was set on fire. Although proof was lacking, most whites in Mashpee were quick to assume that Indians were behind the vandalism and the arson. Town officials even issued warnings about the possibility of violence by the summertime if the lawsuit was not settled quickly. However, attempts to achieve an out-of-court settlement came to nothing. Early in 1977, the Indians offered to drop their claim to all developed property in exchange for most of the town's thirteen thousand acres of undeveloped land—including bodies of water and access to shorelines—which would then be preserved for recreation, hunting, and fishing. Although the proposal had some support from environmentalists, it was rejected by the town selectmen, the real-estate developers, and a majority of the non-Indian homeowners, who, without making a counterproposal, demanded that Congress enact legislation guaranteeing them full and clear title to their property.

The Indians, seeking to convince the whites that their basic objective was not to displace homeowners but to prevent further development, voluntarily amended their suit in August 1977, to exempt all private homes and accompanying land of an acre or less. This reduced the total amount of real estate they claimed to about eleven thousand acres. That same month, William B. Gunter, a retired Georgia Supreme Court justice who had been studying the situation in Mashpee since April as President Carter's special representative for Indian land claims, withdrew from the case. Judge Gunter said he could find no viable solution to the dispute, and he recommended that the question of whether the Mashpees were a tribe proceed to court. In September, a suggestion by Gunter that a federal mediator be appointed—a proposal welcomed by the Indians—was turned down by the selectmen, and they also refused to approve last-minute legislation to resolve the matter, which was proposed to the Senate's Select Subcommittee on Indian Affairs by Senator Edward M. Kennedy, Senator Edward Brooke, and Representative Gerry Studds. This legislation would have given clear title to all lands occupied by private homes or businesses in return for a payment of four million dollars by the federal government to the Mashpees, and at no cost whatever to the town of Mashpee or the Commonwealth of Massachusetts. Moreover, the subcommittee was prepared to act favorably on the measure if the selectmen, two of whom had been in the real-estate business, had been willing to give their approval.

The long-awaited trial began on October 17th, lasted through the end of the year, and proved to be tremendously complex. From the beginning, lawyers for the Mashpees argued before Judge Walter J. Skinner that he should accept as the legal definition of a tribe one that had been handed down by the Supreme Court in 1901, in the case of Montoya v. the United States, which concerned the Apache Tribe in New Mexico. In that decision, the Court had defined an Indian tribe as "a body of Indians of the same or a similar race, united in a community under one leadership or government, and inhabiting a particular, though sometimes ill-defined, territory." Lawyers for the defense argued that, since the land claim was based upon an alleged violation of the federal Nonintercourse Act of 1790, the Judge should accept as the legal definition of a tribe the one that was generally understood at that time, which, they claimed, stressed the concept of sovereignty and political autonomy.

Lawrence Shubow, the attorney NARF had retained to argue the case for the plaintiffs, declared in his opening statement to the jury that the Mashpees would show they were a tribe by proving that they were people of Indian ancestry who considered themselves Indian and were considered Indians by the outside world; that they had lived in Mashpee for more than three hundred and fifty years; that during this time they had made up a cohesive, permanent community with a common heritage and many shared ways of living; and that they had always had their own form of organization and leadership. St. Clair countered by telling the judge and jury that the federal government had never recognized the Mashpees as a sovereign Indian tribe; that the disputed land had not been granted to Wampanoags to begin with but to a mixed group of Indians, who after being converted to Christianity had left the Wampanoag Federation and become assimilated; that many of the Indian customs in Mashpee were of comparatively recent origin; and that because of intermarriage over two centuries the jury would have to decide whether the Mashpees had always considered themselves Indians or whether they had come to consider themselves blacks.

During the thirty-eight days of testimony that followed, the jury heard a welter of conflicting evidence as witnesses for both sides described and analyzed the history of the Mashpees over the last three centuries. Testifying on behalf of the plaintiffs, Dr. James Axtell, a visiting professor of history at Northwestern University and a National Endowment for the Humanities research fellow at the Newberry Library, in Chicago, declared that the Mashpees had been a tribe in 1870 and were a tribe at the present time, because of their ancestry, Indian nature, and social organization. Axtell went on to say that the Mashpees had survived because the earliest deeds gave them land that could not be sold without the full consent of everyone in the tribe; because they had accepted Christianity as a protective cover and had avoided becoming involved in King Philip's War; and because they had been able to run their own affairs at given points in their history, which, in turn, had allowed them to develop their own leaders. On the other hand, Dr. Francis G. Hutchins, a political scientist from Harvard who had been a fellow at the Newberry Library's Center for the History of the American Indian, testified that the Mashpees had not been a tribe since the sixteen-fifties, when they voluntarily placed themselves under the laws and jurisdiction of Plymouth Colony. Dr. Hutchins also offered the opinion that the failure of the Mashpees to pack up and move West after King Philip's War constituted a voluntary abandonment of tribal status.

Another witness for the plaintiff was Dr. Jack Campisi, an anthropologist from the State University of New York at New Paltz, who testified that the Mashpees of today were a tribe, and whose definition of one closely paralleled the Supreme Court's Montoya decision: a closely knit and extensive kinship system comprising a community, some form of political leadership, and an indigenous concept of homeland. Dr. Campisi's definition was strongly supported by Dr. William

Sturtevant, who is curator of North American ethnology at the National Museum of the Smithsonian Institution and adjunct professor of anthropology at Johns Hopkins University. Dr. Sturtevant testified that the tribal characteristics found by Dr. Campisi in the Mashpees were common and could be seen in all groups of Indians in the United States. On the other hand, Dr. Jeanne Guillemin, a professor of sociology at Boston College, testified for the defense that in her opinion the Indian community in Mashpee did not constitute a tribe because it did not have an independent political organization or economic autonomy and because it was not culturally distinct.

Throughout the trial, St. Clair and Allan van Gestel, an attorney engaged by a group of land-title insurance companies to represent the interests of clients owning land in Mashpee, strongly challenged the Mashpees' claim to tribal status on the ground that the Indians lacked a separate government and an independent leadership with strong authority over tribal members. (Van Gestel would later represent Jacqueline Kennedy Onassis and other Indian land-claim defendants in Gay Head, on Martha's Vineyard.) To prove their contention that the Mashpees were not a tribe, St. Clair and van Gestel called a number of Indians to the witness stand and elicited from them testimony that they did not consider Earl Mills and other tribal officials to be their political leaders. Shubow argued that a continuing leadership provided by a network of closely interrelated families had existed in Mashpee for three hundred and fifty years, and that whether the Indian leaders were called sachems or selectmen made little difference. When Earl Mills testified, he described his own leadership of the Mashpees as follows: "I have no power over anybody. I carry out their will. We operate by consensus."

Predictably, perhaps, the question of race became an issue in the trial. Most of the Mashpees who were called to the stand traced their ancestry to people listed as Indians in a census taken by the Commonwealth of Massachusetts in 1859. As a result, the jury kept hearing over and over again the old Mashpee family names of Pocknett, Attaquin, Webquish, Queppish, Amos, Peters, Mills, and Oakley, which can be found on the stones of the graveyard beside the meetinghouse. St. Clair, however, pointedly referred to the Mashpees as "persons with a reputation for some Indian ancestry," and continually raised the subject of miscegenation in cross-examination, which brought charges from some quarters that he was pursuing a racist strategy. A typical example occurred during his questioning of Selena Coombs, a sixty-year-old woman whose great-great-uncle was Joseph Amos, the blind Baptist preacher, and whose name is believed to have been derived from Hiacoomes, an early Christian convert from Martha's Vineyard. After Mrs. Coombs had testified about traditional Indian dishes such as sheldrake stew, eel stifle, a stew called potato bargain, and cornmeal dumplings, St. Clair pointed out to her that the censuses of 1849 and 1859 contained different descriptions of the racial origins of some of the Mashpees.

"When you say Indian, you mean a person you believe has some Indian blood," he told Mrs. Coombs.

"I didn't come here to talk about blood quantums," she replied.

St. Clair had already brought up the matter of racial intermarriage with Vernon Pocknett, a forty-four-year-old shellfishermen who was reseeding the shellfish beds in Poponesset Bay, in South Mashpee, with the aid of a federal grant. Pocknett is a nephew of Mabel Avant and a descendant of the Indian sachem Paupmunnuck, who in 1648 sold what is now the town of Barnstable to Miles Standish for two brass kettles and a hoe. During cross-examination, St. Clair confronted him with the fact that town records of 1897 identified the race of one of his grandfathers with the letter "M," for mulatto.

"Do you recognize the letter 'M' as indicating mulatto in the town's records?" St. Clair asked.

"I don't know what mulatto is," Pocknett answered.

Shubow countered by exhibiting the 1859 state census, which identified Pocknett's great-grandfather as Indian. He pointed out that the English had referred to the Mashpees as blacks since before the Revolutionary War, and that census-takers had often repeated the error throughout the nineteenth century. The jury learned that for years it was a practice at the Falmouth High School that Mashpee Indian girls had to take household arts and Mashpee boys went into agriculture. The jury also was told that during the first part of this century no fewer than ten Mashpees had attended the federal Indian school at Carlisle, Pennsylvania. In addition, a professional genealogist testified that she had carefully checked the ancestry of the present members of the tribe back to the 1859 census, and that every Mashpee selectman from 1834 to 1964 either was an Indian or was married to an Indian. Ultimately, the question of whether St. Clair should have injected the racial issue into the trial to begin with was placed in doubt by the testimony of another witness for the plaintiff, Vine Deloria, Jr., an Oglala Sioux, who is a lawyer and the author of the book "Custer

Died for Your Sins." Deloria told the jury that some federally recognized tribes had no full-blooded Indians whatever.

In his closing statement, St. Clair continued to hammer away at
what he obviously considered the two weakest points in the Mashpee's
claim to be a tribe—the question of racial mixture and the question
of whether there had been continuous political leadership among them.
Of their being Indian, he was openly skeptical, if not downright scorn-
ful. "I suspect that some of that belief has become more pronounced
in the last couple of years," he declared. "In any event, it is clear that
some people having an option to decide whether or not they were
Portuguese, black, mulatto, or a whole variety of other races have
elected to consider themselves at least part Indian." St. Clair went
on to tell the jury that belief of partial Indian ancestry on the part of
the Mashpees was not sufficient to warrant their claim. As for tribal
status, he said that when Mashpee was incorporated, in 1870, the
inhabitants did not have the slightest idea that they constituted an
Indian tribe. St. Clair described Earl Mills as a ceremonial figurehead,
who could not even control beer-drinking at the annual powwows,
and he made light of efforts to assert cultural identity in terms of
Indian dishes such as cornmeal dumplings and potato bargain. He
concluded by telling the jury that "last-minute efforts to create the
appearance of a tribe won't do the trick," and that the fact that a lot
of people in Mashpee are related to one another does not make the
place "really different from any other small rural community."

Shubow began his closing argument by asking the jurors if they
had been told of any other rural community in Massachusetts where
two hundred adults and their children had been living in a network
of closely related families for more than three hundred years. He went
on to remind them that the word "tribe" was not Indian but English
in origin; that it was not employed in America until 1750; but that
from then on it was applied regularly to the Mashpees both by the
Mashpees and by their white neighbors. As for the question of leadership, Shubow pointed out that the government of the Mashpees had
always rested in the family structure of the community; that the political leadership of the Indians resembled that of the New England
town meeting; and that the tribal chief therefore did not rule with an
iron hand but carried out the will of the people. Concerning Earl
Mills' alleged inability to control beer-drinking at the powwows, Shubow remarked that he was "struck by Jimmy Carter's problem with
Billy Carter," and told the jury that it was not a fair test of leadership

to require a leader to exhibit absolute power every day of the week. Shubow, who later became a Massachusetts State court judge, admitted that it was difficult at first for him to accept the idea that an Indian tribe could exist on Cape Cod in 1977, but said that the difficulty arose only because Americans were conditioned to think of Indians in terms of unrealistic stereotypes. He also told the jurors that there had been a hidden appeal to racial prejudice in the case, which should be brushed aside as irrelevant. After reviewing the long epic of the Mashpees, Shubow declared that their survival was a social miracle, and that it had occurred because of the determination, will, and leadership of the Indian community. "Don't deny these people their identity," he said. "They have done nothing to deserve such a fate at the hands of jurors. They have been fighting for their identity for three hundred and fifty years."

From the beginning of the trial, it had been clear that Judge Skinner's charge to the jury would be crucial to the outcome, since it was up to him to instruct the jurors in how they should go about determining whether the Mashpees were an Indian tribe. On January 4th, 1978, the day after St. Clair and Shubow made their closing statements, the judge delivered his charge in a discursive three-hour speech that contained many of his own opinions on the evidence and issues in the case. To begin with, he read the formal questions of the charge, telling the jurors that they must decide whether the Mashpees were a tribe on any of six specific dates—the earliest being July 22, 1790, when Congress passed the first version of the Nonintercourse Act, and the latest being August 26, 1976, when the Mashpees filed their lawsuit—and that if they found that the Mashpees were a tribe on any of the dates before 1976 they must also determine whether the tribe existed continuously from that point on. He then said that the burden of proof was on the plaintiffs, and that if the jurors were in doubt on any particular issue they must find for the defendants. Judge Skinner had already informed lawyers for both sides about his feelings in this regard, saying he believed that the land claim of the Mashpees was a radical remedy for the alleged wrong. "It seems to me quite proper to say that whoever seeks that remedy has got to show that they are in a radically different kind of status than other people," he told them.

After reviewing the testimony of the witnesses, Skinner continued his charge by instructing the jurors that the essential definition for the existence of an Indian tribe was to be found in Montoya v. the United States: "a body of Indians of the same or a similar race, united in a community under one leadership or government, and inhabiting a particular, though sometimes ill-defined territory." He then examined the various elements of this definition. Concerning the question of whether the Mashpees were really Indians, he began by telling the jurors that he had been very surprised, when he read through Montoya, to find Supreme Court justices talking at the turn of the century about the natural infirmities of the Indian character—that such language demonstrated the essentially racist nature of the American attitude toward the Indians, and that its use in the highest court in the land could only have reflected an enormous prejudice in the streets and villages of the nation. For this reason, he cautioned the jurors not to be surprised to find Indians and blacks lumped together in old census records and other documents pertaining to the Mashpees. Concerning St. Clair's attempts to assert that intermarriage between Mashpees and blacks had disqualified the Mashpees from consideration as Indians, Skinner declared that such intermarriage was both normal and natural, and that if it had not occurred an impermissible level of inbreeding would have resulted. "The question is a question of fact and not of law," he told the jury. "On the evidence, are you satisfied that the tribal existence survived, and that the outsiders were incorporated into the tribe and became part of it?"

Judge Skinner went on to comment on the requirement in the Montoya definition that there be an Indian community, saying that such a community had to have some cultural boundary separating it from the surrounding society. He observed that during certain periods in Mashpee history—particularly between 1870 and 1920— the evidence for this was scanty. When he came to the requirement that the Indians inhabit a particular territory, he digressed by reminding the jurors that conquest was the basis for every land title in the United States, and telling them that "we cannot simply ignore the existence of a rather elaborate civilization at this point." He then described the land deeded in common to the Indians and their children by Plymouth Colony as an estate of entailment—referring to the restriction that none of the land could legally be sold without the consent of all the Indians. After noting that part of the entailment was removed in 1842, when the Massachusetts legislators authorized formal partition of the Mashpee District lands among the Indians, and that the rest of the entailment was abolished in 1869, when the legislature for the first time allowed the Mashpees to sell their lands to non-Indians, Skinner told the jurors that they must decide whether, in accepting this property, the Indians intended to give up their tribal status and accept an English form of government or whether it was simply a question of the tribe's carrying on as property owners under a different label. Commenting upon abandonment and the necessity for historical continuity, he declared that "once tribal status has been voluntarily abandoned, it is my opinion that it is lost and cannot be revived." As for the opinion offered by Francis Hutchins that the failure of the Mashpees to pack up and go West after King Philip's War constituted voluntary abandonment, Judge Skinner dismissed this out of hand. "I instruct you that that is not a permissible inference as a matter of law, because there were too many other considerations," he told the jury, adding that the Indians obviously had no free choice in the matter, considering the hazard of warfare with the whites, the risk of encountering bounty hunters, and the fact that their entire economy was based on shellfish and herring, which were not to be found in the Western forests.

Far and away the most important part of Judge Skinner's charge centered on the question of leadership and government. After a digression into the history of the concept of sovereignty, he concluded that Indian tribes had been deprived of any real sovereignty from the time they were subjected by the Europeans, but he told the jurors that sovereignty, or the lack of it, really had no bearing on the matter of tribal existence. He then instructed the jury that what was applicable in the case of the Mashpees was whether a concept of leadership that derived from a once independent Indian political community had continued and whether it had substantially governed the Indians' internal affairs. He also offered the opinion that, except when the Indians had filed certain petitions, evidence of political leadership in the early days of the Mashpees was scarce.

As for the leadership existing in Mashpee today, Skinner reiterated his belief that in order to satisfy the definition in Montoya it must exercise some measure of control over the internal affairs of the people. "For the leadership to be such as qualified the group as a tribe, there must be followers," he declared. He appeared to be unimpressed by the contention of the Mashpees that their leaders were leaders with respect to a way of life, and even told the jury that he found the testimony in that connection to be neither very strong nor very full.

"You must find that the leadership, whatever it is, has a significant effect upon a majority of the group," he said.

Considering the complexity of the case, few observers were surprised when the jury came back two days later with the finding that the Mashpees had been a tribe on some of the dates in question but not on others. What no one expected, however, was the specific way in which the jury split its verdict. Attorneys for the plaintiffs were especially puzzled as to how the jurors could decide that the Mashpees were a tribe in 1834 and 1842 but not in 1790, since this finding seemed not only to defy any historically logical point of view but also to contradict Judge Skinner's instruction that once tribal status had been abandoned it could not be revived. Shubow went as far as to speculate that the jurors may have wished to acknowledge existence of a tribe at some point, but not on the significant date of July 22, 1790, since acknowledging its existence then would have been to acknowledge that the lands of the Mashpees were under the protection of Congress, and would have provided powerful substantiation of the Indians' claim that their territory had later been taken from them illegally. For their part, lawyers for the defendants seemed to feel that the key date in determining the outcome was 1976. By voting that no tribe existed then, they claimed, the jurors had found that no one had been entitled to bring suit in the first place.

In spite of the fact that the verdict appeared damaging to the cause of the plaintiffs, Judge Skinner did not dismiss the Mashpees' lawsuit then and there but gave their attorneys several weeks to show why he should not enter a judgment of dismissal. On January 26th, opposition to entry of judgment was argued before him by Barry Margolin, of the Native American Rights Fund, who declared at the outset that the special verdicts returned by the jury were irreconcilably inconsistent and could not represent a correct application of the law to the evidence. Margolin pointed out that the jury had found the proprietors of Mashpee to have been an Indian tribe between 1834 and 1842 and for an undertermined period between 1790 and 1869. Margolin reasoned that, since it was undisputed that between 1790 and 1869 the Indian proprietors owned most of Mashpee in common, the land came under the protection of the United States as the Nonintercourse Act stipulated. He then argued that, since the jury decided that the Mashpees were not a tribe in 1869, and since there had been no congressional action terminating the tribe, this decision could be based only upon a finding that the Mashpees had voluntarily abandoned their tribal status between 1842 and 1869.

At this point, Margolin cited a number of court decisions to prove his contention that abandonment was a precise legal term, signifying an act of absolute and deliberate relinquishment; that it could never be presumed but must be proved by unequivocal and decisive evidence; and that voluntary abandonment of tribal status must reflect the intent of the entire tribe. He went on to say that the jury's decision concerning the Mashpees was the first finding by any federal court in history that a tribe had voluntarily abandoned its status without action by Congress, and he added that no reasoned view of the evidence could support such a finding. As proof of this, Margolin argued that the only major changes that had taken place in Mashpee between 1842 and 1869 were the partitioning of most of the proprietors' lands under the state act of 1842, and the removal of sale restrictions on the partitioned tracts under the state act of 1869. "These events could not, as a matter of law, support the finding of tribal abandonment," he declared. "The Supreme Court has consistently held that the allotment of tribal lands and the grant of citizenship to tribal members do not affect the tribal status of the Indians or Congress's continuing authority over them."

Arguing that the jury's findings for 1842 and 1869 were in fundamental conflict and could not both be correct, Margolin went on to tell Skinner that, since the findings for 1870 and 1976 were dependent upon the finding for 1869, they were invalid. By the same token, he said, the jury's finding for 1790 could not be reconciled with its finding for 1834, since the court had instructed the jury that once a tribe was dissolved it could not emerge again. After pointing out that the court had broad discretion to refuse to accept jury answers that resulted from confusion or inconsistency, Margolin told Skinner that the Indians were entitled to expect that their claims would be resolved on the basis of an objective and rational evaluation of the issues. He then made an observation that went far beyond the case at hand: "A judgment based on these self-contradictory special verdicts would be a rejection of the plaintiff's claim for justice, not because the plaintiff was wrong but simply because the claims were too hard for the legal system to resolve."

A few days after Margolin had put forward his argument, I visited a friend—an attorney who lives in Boston and who had been following the trial since its beginning—and asked his opinion of how things had gone. "There's an old saying that hard cases make bad law," he replied. "What that means is that when the court is overly worried about the consequences of a ruling, it often changes the rules to avoid the consequences. Theoretically, of course, the court is not supposed to change the rules because it doesn't like the consequences of the law. The court is supposed to be neutral, and the law is supposed to be blind."

My attorney friend went on to say that in the case of the Mashpees what the court was supposed to do was not to consider the consequences of applying the federal Nonintercourse Act of 1790 but to rule on whether it had been violated. "For this reason, Judge Skinner may have committed a serious error when he informed counsel for both sides at the end of the trial that because of the severity of the remedy being sought by the Mashpees he had decided to put a heavier than ordinary burden of proof upon them," he declared. "He may have made another error when he told the jury, in effect, that there wasn't much leadership in Mashpee. In fact, he may have erroneously directed a judgment against the Indians."

On the same day, I paid a call on Barry Margolin in a temporary office that had been opened by the Native American Rights Fund in a building just across the street from the federal courthouse, on Post Office Square, in downtown Boston. A tall, bespectacled man of twenty-eight, Margolin was wearing a pair of baggy bluejeans and a white shirt that had come partly untucked. When I asked him how he felt Judge Skinner would rule on the objections he had made to a judgment of dismissal, he smiled and shrugged and said he expected the decision to go against him. "It is obvious that there was no basis for a finding of voluntary abandonment by 1869," he continued. "So it is obvious that the jurors either did not understand the court's instructions or didn't understand the evidence. As for Judge Skinner, he is caught on the horns of a considerable dilemma. He can't give the case back to the jury for further consideration, because the jurors have gone home. He can't enter findings in place of the jury, because the defendants refused to waive trial by jury. He can't wait for the Department of the Interior to decide on the case, because he has already rejected that solution. And he isn't likely to order a new trial, because that would be too expensive and time-consuming. Which doesn't leave him with much choice, does it? My bet is that he will dismiss the case and risk being overturned on appeal."

As it turned out, Margolin's assessment was right. On March 24th, Judge Skinner rejected the argument that the special verdicts were inconsistent, and dismissed the lawsuit, declaring that the jury's answer was "perfectly rational and does not reflect a lack of understanding." In his written opinion, Judge Skinner elaborated on his earlier interpretation that the Nonintercourse Act of 1790 placed a particularly heavy burden of proof upon the plaintiffs. "The standards of that Act, at least as I have interpreted it, require that a tribe demonstrate a definable organization before it can qualify for the extraordinary remedy of the total voiding of land titles acquired in good faith and without fraud," he wrote.

On March 24th, Judge Skinner also rejected a motion by lawyers for the defense, who had filed for a directed verdict in their favor on the ground that the protection of the Nonintercourse Act did not apply to Indians who, like the Mashpees, were living on land surrounded by settlements of citizens of the United States. The judge pointed out that a defense based upon "the so-called white-settlement exception" had already been rejected by a court ruling in the 1976 case of the Narragansett Tribe of Indians v. the Southern Rhode Island Land Development Corporation.

In the meantime, there had been a startling and unpublicized development in the case. On March 8th, Judge Skinner received a communication from an attorney who was a resident of Falmouth, and who said that he had discussed the case with one of the jurors, who also lived in Falmouth, while the trial was still in progress. Judge Skinner called an evidentiary hearing for the next day, at which time the lawyer who had sent the communication told the court that the juror had stated that he had received an anonymous telephone call in which the caller said, "You know how you'd better vote." On March 10th, the juror in question appeared before Judge Skinner and counsel for both sides, and testified that he had, indeed, received an anonymous phone call, telling him, "You know which way you better go"; that he had mentioned the call to his fellow-townsman but that he had not acted on the attorney's advice to report the incident. Judge

Skinner refused to conduct an investigation into whether the threat-ened juror had discussed the telephone call with his fellow-jurors, or whether any of them had received similar calls. He decided that the call had not unduly influenced the juror and that it "did not impeach the jury's verdict in any way at all." He then ordered the investigation into the matter closed, and said that he would deny any motion for a new trial or a mistrial predicated on any of the evidence presented at the hearing.

In spite of Judge Skinner's ruling, the question of possible jury tampering in the Mashpee case was not laid to rest. On August 31st, in an appeal brief filed before the United States Court of Appeals for the First Circuit, Barry Margolin; Thomas Tureen, who had by then taken responsibility for the appeal; and Richard Collins and Moshe Genauer, two more NARF lawyers, sought to have Judge Skinner's dismissal of the Indians' lawsuit reversed by arguing that the judge had failed to conduct a thorough investigation into an unlawful attempt to influence the jury by curtailing the evidentiary hearing and by refusing to allow questioning of the other jurors in the matter. The lawyers for the Mashpees also argued that Judge Skinner had erred in failing to defer to the jurisdiction of the Department of the Interior on the issue of tribal existence; in instructing the jury that a tribe must have a continuous leadership with binding authority over tribal mem-bers; and in refusing to instruct the jury that a tribe could cease to exist only through complete and voluntary abandonment of its tribal organization. Pointing out that the special verdicts returned by the jury were "irreconcilably inconsistent and fatally ambiguous," counsel for the Mashpees called upon the United States Court of Appeals for the First Circuit to reverse Judge Skinner, to remand for a new trial, and to order the proceedings stayed pending the outcome of a deter-mination by the Department of the Interior on the question of tribal status.

On October 10th, St. Clair, van Gestel, and lawyers for the New Seabury Corporation, and the other defendants filed a brief denying the validity of all of the assertions in the plaintiffs' brief. Concerning the charge of possible jury tampering, they argued that under the law the court had complete discretion to determine the extent and type of investigation into the matter; that Judge Skinner was not, therefore, required to hold a full evidentiary hearing; and that he had "properly denied the plaintiff's request to conduct a 'fishing expedition.' "

The question of whether the Nonintercourse Act of 1790 and the other Trade and Intercourse Acts that were subsequently passed by Congress applied to the Mashpees was the subject of still another set of briefs filed before the Court of Appeals. St. Clair and his colleagues argued that Judge Skinner had erred in denying their motion for a directed verdict in their favor on the ground that the Mashpees and their lands did not fall under the coverage of the Trade and Intercourse Acts and their land-trading provisions. According to the lawyers for the defense, these laws "specifically exempted Indians living on lands surrounded by settlements of citizens of the United States and within the jurisdiction of a state."

In their answering brief, Tureen and his colleagues asserted that the citizen-settlement exception applied only to transactions involving nontribal lands. They went on to point out that a defense based on the citizen-settlement exception had already been rejected by the court in the case of the Narragansett Tribe, and that in any event the Mashpee lands were "no more surrounded by citizen settlements than were most, if not all, of eastern reservations in the nineteenth century, including, for example, the reservations in New York."

During the previous winter, I had gone back to Mashpee to see how the Indians were bearing up under the disappointment of Judge Skinner's dismissal of their lawsuit, and what they were planning for the future. On a clear, cold morning at the end of February, I spent several hours with Ramona Peters—a great-granddaughter of Mabel Avant, who had died in 1964. The Peters family has played a prominent role in Mashpee affairs over the years. Ramona's grandfather, Steven Peters, was a selectman for almost twenty-five years; her father, John Peters, who is a retired contractor, was the tribe's medicine man from 1956 until 1977, when he became supreme medicine man of all the Wampanoags; her aunt Amelia Peters Bingham was tremendously influential during the early nineteen-seventies in reviving the Mashpees' interest in their history; and her uncle Russell Peters, who was then president of the Mashpee Wampanoag Indian Tribal Council, Incorporated, had been a prime mover behind the lawsuit. Ramona, who was twenty-six at the time I met her was a quiet, intense woman with long, dark hair. A graduate of the University of Arizona, she was teaching Indian history and culture to children of Wampanoag descent at the Mashpee elementary school under a grant from the Department of Health, Education, and Wel-

*Bernard Coombs; Ambrose Pells; Oaks A. Coombs, Jr.,
retired whaler and former chief of the Mashpee Wampanoags, at
the age of 82; Amelia Peters Bingham at the age of 14; Isadora
Pells; Steven A. Peters, Jr., age 13, who was killed in action in
Normandy, in 1944. Photograph taken in 1937.*

fare. She was also working with her father to revive interest in the Indian religion in Mashpee. "There's a great rejuvenation going on here,"she told me. "It's what Indians call preparing for Purification Time. By practicing rituals such as burning tobacco, offering thanks for all living things, and attending the naming ceremonies, we can protect our Indian identity and provide an alternative to the Christian system."

When I asked her what the effect of losing the lawsuit might be, she took a deep breath and shook her head. "There could be violence," she said quickly. "Everything is out in the open now. There has even been talk among the whites of bringing in the Ku Klux Klan and the John Birch Society. All I know is that if no remedy is provided, Mashpee will be a divided community forever." At this point, Ramona Peters paused. "Who knows?" she said wistfully. "If those of us who are tradition-minded find ourselves without a land base, perhaps we could go to the Penobscot territory."

That evening, I paid a call on her uncle Russell Peters, who then lived on Route 28, not far from the old meetinghouse. He is a stocky man in his late forties with a forthright, urbane manner, and he had just returned from Boston, where he worked as director of a federally financed television series on southern New England Indians. "The decision of the jury was political, not legal," he told me. "Can you imagine an all-white jury ruling in favor of Indians against an all-white group of landowners? As for Judge Skinner, he rationalized over the harsh remedy we were seeking, and conveniently forgot how harsh our history had been. Of course, we'll have to appeal the jury's verdict. A tribe without land is no tribe at all. Meanwhile, we've rallied our people and made our cause known to the public. That's an accomplishment in itself. Who ever heard of us until we filed suit?"

When I returned to Mashpee to keep an appointment with Earl Mills a few days later, I drove over the same road I had taken on my first visit. Along the way, I noticed some changes—a motel, a garage, and half a dozen dwellings that had not been there before. In the center of the village, there were some other changes. The little frame post office was gone; the ramshackle fire station wore a sign saying that it had been condemned and the Ockry Trading Post had become a liquor store. Farther up the road, Mabel Avant's house had been spruced up and now wore a sign proclaiming it as the Mashpee Wampanoag Indian Museum. Inside were the usual artifacts—some Indian baskets, several bows and arrows, a cradle board, and an assortment of stone arrowheads, axes, tomahawks, and sharpening tools—and in the front room, above a fireplace, hung a primitive painting of Richard Bourne preaching to an alfresco gathering of Indians under the famous oak tree.

After visiting the museum, I drove back down the road, crossed the herring run, and turned in at a drive leading up behind Mill Pond to a restaurant called The Flume, which Earl had built seven years before and named after the sluiceway that flows out of nearby Mashpee-Wakeby Pond. I had not seem him for even longer than that, and when he opened the door of the upstairs apartment, where he was living, the first thing that struck me was how little he had changed. Of course, there had been changes other than physical, and for the first few minutes of our meeting we sat at the kitchen table and brought each other up to date. During the interval, he had been divorced and remarried, and had become the father of a daughter, now six years old, who came bounding into the room and asked him to fix her hair. While he busied himself brushing and braiding, he told me that his mother and father had died, and that Elwoood had sold the trading post and left town in the autumn of 1976. "Elwood couldn't take the changes that had come in Mashpee," Earl said. "He couldn't fish where he wanted anymore, and that helped drive him out. These days, he lives in a cabin on top of a hill in the Rangeley Lakes district, in Maine. He doesn't often come back."

When I asked Earl how he felt about the trial, he told me he thought the Mashpees had shown themselves well under difficult circumstances. As for losing the lawsuit, he was not as upset as I imagined he might be, nor did he speculate on the outcome of the appeals that would be made. "The main thing is that there has been a new awakening among us," he said. "A new awareness of our heritage. A sudden nudge. Like a gust of wind on a sailboat. Soon our people will wake up to the fact that we still have a lot of land here and many other resources."

A year later, the new awakening that Earl Mills perceived among the Mashpees gave way to resignation, bitterness, and despair when the appeals were lost and the Indians realized that they had been defeated once again. Oral argument in the appeal of Mashpee Tribe v. New Seabury Corporation took place on November 8, 1978; on February 13, 1979, a three-judge panel of the United States Court of Appeals for the First Circuit upheld the jury's verdict. At the outset of their opinion, the three jurists acknowledged that the question of whether the Mashpees were a legally constituted tribe posed a considerable dilemma. "This issue is particularly difficult in this case because the Mashpees differ from most other groups who have sought to assert rights as Indian tribes," they declared. "The federal government has never officially recognized the Mashpees as a tribe or actively supported or watched over them. Moreover, the Mashpees have a long history of intermarriage with non-Indians and acceptance of non-Indian religion and culture. These facts do not necessarily mean that the Mashpees are not a tribe protected by federal law, but they do make the issue of tribal existence a difficult factual question for the jury."

In upholding the verdict for the defendants, the appeals court judges said that the jury had obviously found that between 1842 and 1869 the Mashpees had decided to abandon their tribal rights and status voluntarily, and to assimilate with the rest of society. They also ruled that the jury had followed the law in so deciding. They went on to declare that "though a few isolated sentences of the charge may have been unclear or overstated," Judge Skinner's instructions were largely consistent with the plaintiffs' own view of the law. Two of the three judges then revealed just how narrow the scope of their assessment of Skinner's charge had been. "Because there are no sure yardsticks against which to measure the court's instructions, we cannot say that even those we considered are correct or the best possible, but we have not found any law conflicting with the portion of the charge we have reviewed," they declared. (The third judge issued a separate concurring opinion on this point, saying that he believed Skinner's instructions on the definition of a tribe to be legally correct, and should be relied upon in future cases.) As for the argument that Skinner had failed to investigate sufficiently the possible impact on the jury of the anonymous phone call that had been made to one of its members, the First Circuit judges decided that "Although the trial court's inquiry was terminated too soon to have been fully satisfactory," Skinner had acted within the bounds of his discretion in concluding it when he had. Given the unanimity of the First Circuit's opinion, it was highly unlikely that the Supreme Court would consent to hear an appeal of its decision, and this proved to be the case. On October 1, 1979, the high court denied the Mashpees' petition for writ of certiorari, and Mashpee Tribe v. New Seabury Corporation finally came to an end.

During 1980, the Mashpees hired new attorneys who claimed that Tureen, Margolin, and NARF had been mistaken in trying to prove that they were a tribe within the Montoya definition, and who set out to establish that the Nonintercourse Act protected individual Indians as well as Indian tribes. As a result, in December of 1981, a new land-claim lawsuit, known as Mashpee II, was brought in federal district court by three hundred and thirty-four individual members of the Mashpee Tribe. However, it was dismissed in June of 1982 by Judge Skinner on the grounds that it was clearly barred by the jury verdict in Mashpee Tribe v. New Seabury. Skinner's decision was affirmed by the First Circuit appellate court in May of 1983, and in October the Supreme Court refused to hear the case.

As might be expected, this second setback did little to raise the morale of the Mashpees, who had now virtually exhausted their legal remedies for regaining any of their lost territory. To make matters worse, their self-esteem was soon delivered a gratuitous blow, when the *Wall Street Journal* ran a front-page story on the day before Thanksgiving, carrying a headline that read, "Time Hasn't Blessed Indians Who Shared 'First Thanksgiving,' " and a sub-head that read, "Wampanoags, Few and Poor, Can't Even Convince Some That They're Still a Tribe." The author of the *Journal* article started out by saying that there were only about twenty-five hundred Wampanoags left in New England, that none of them could speak their native language, and that many of them were "unemployed school dropouts." He went on to deliver some highly questionable pronouncements. "For years, the Wampanoags called themselves Negroes, or 'colored,' " he de-clared, apparently unaware that the Mashpees and other Wampanoag descendants had almost never referred to themselves in this manner, but had been designated as black, mulatto, Negro, colored, or Indian in a variety of state and federal censuses that had been taken over a hundred-year period by enumerators who were obviously uncertain about how to categorize them. Compounding this error, he then said that in rejecting the Mashpees' claim for ancestral lands, a federal court had ruled that "because of years of intermarriage and assimila-tion, the Wampanoags aren't really an Indian tribe." The federal court had, of course, done no such thing. It had decided that the Mashpees were not a tribe, not on the grounds of intermarriage or miscegenation, but because a jury had found that the Mashpees had voluntarily aban-doned their tribal status between 1842 and 1869.

Sad to say, there was nothing new about the *Journal*'s denigration of the Mashpees. Indeed, it had become a tradition over more than two hundred and fifty years. It had begun at the beginning of the eighteenth century when the Massachusetts Bay Colony had sent overseers to manage their affairs; it had continued into the nineteenth century, when the Reverend James Freeman had described their meetinghouse as "a cage of unclean birds"; it had persisted in 1930, when Henry C. Kittredge, son of the famous Shakespearean scholar George Lyman Kittredge, published a book entitled "Cape Cod, Its People and Their History," in which he declared that the Mashpees' tax-free status had "brought the scum of the Indian and Negro population from all over the State drifting into Mashpee like weeds to the Sargasso Sea"; and, of course, it had been present in the racial undertones and innuendoes which marked the trial that had taken place in Judge Skinner's court in the autumn of 1977 and early winter of 1978. As for the *Journal*'s role in its continuation, little remains to be said except that the editors of the newspaper declined to print a letter from the members of the Mashpee Wampanoag Indian Tribal Council, who pointed out the errors and protested the aspersions in the article.

In February of 1984, the Tribal Council elected Vernon Pocknett as its new president. It was an event that many friends of the Mashpees found hopeful, for in spite of the fact that Pocknett has little formal education—he left school after the eighth grade—he is an outspoken and committed man, who is much admired in Mashpee for having stood up to St. Clair under cross-examination in the 1977–78 trial. During the spring, Pocknett urged his fellow Mashpees to ask NARF to petition the Department of the Interior for federal tribal recognition under a set of recently promulgated regulations which set forth standards for determining tribal status, and during the early summer the Mashpees voted overwhelmingly to do so. (In 1983, under this same procedure, the government had recognized the Narragansetts, whose history and situation are very similar to those of the Mashpees, and no legal impediment exists to prevent it from doing the same for the Mashpees, because the United States was not a party to Mashpee v. New Seabury and is not bound by the decision in the case.)

Pocknett also became involved in a long-smouldering dispute between Massachusetts and the Mashpees over whether the Indians should be subject to state shellfishing regulations. (During the first part of this century, the regulations had exempted Indians, but when they were amended in the nineteen-forties, the exemption was omitted.) In the winter of 1984, four Mashpees were given citations by a

Vernon Pocknett, President of the Mashpee Wampanoag
Indian Tribal Council. Photograph by Jerry Berndt.

state game warden for shellfishing without a license and for exceeding the catch limit. In September, Lewis Gurwitz of Cambridge, the attorney for the Indians, argued before Judge Brian Rowe in the First District Court of Barnstable that the Mashpees were exercising their ancestral tribal rights, and cited several recent Supreme Court decisions to prove his point. Gurwitz said that neither state nor local authorities had any jurisdiction over aboriginal hunting and fishing unless the state could prove that there was a conservation need. At the time of the hearing, Pocknett pointed out that there were only about four hundred and fifty members of the Mashpee Tribe living in Mashpee—less than fifteen percent of the town's total year-round population, and only about five percent of its peak summer population—and that since relatively few Indians engaged in shellfishing, they could hardly be considered a threat to the clams and oysters. This argument was persuasive enough to cause the Sunday Cape Cod *Times* to publish an editorial in support of the Mashpees. "The case against the four Indians may be a symbol of the blindness of the law," the newspaper declared. "Indian shellfishing practices present no danger to the resource. Continued refusal by the state to grant them an ancient right—a special privilege, if you will—presents another unnecessary threat to their heritage." Judge Rowe also appeared to have been persuaded. On October 1st, he dismissed the charges against the four Mashpees without giving any reason. Pocknett saw the ruling as a minor victory for his people, pointing out that when Wampanoags had been charged with violating shellfishing regulations in the past, they had always paid the fine rather than challenge the Massachusetts law.

Shortly after Rowe's decision, I drove over to Mashpee from my home on the outer Cape to talk with Pocknett, in order to find out what he had in mind for the Mashpees as president of their Tribal Council. Vernon is a powerfully built, dark-skinned man, now fifty years old, with green eyes, a snaggle-toothed grin, and a ready sense of humor, which goes hand in hand with a deep conviction about the dignity and value of his ancient heritage. (Several years before, while lying seriously injured on a stretcher in the emergency ward of the Falmouth Hospital, following an auto accident, he was asked by a nurse to give his age, whereupon he looked up at her and replied gravely that he was a thousand years old.) On the day I visited him, I found him to be as outspoken as his aunt Mabel Avant had been on the occasion of my first visit to the town, some twenty-two years earlier. "We lost our land and we lost the town, but we aren't going to let Judge Skinner's bad decision keep us down," he told me. "We're going to stand up now and take some steps to preserve our heritage.

They'll have to be small steps at first—like our protest against the shellfishing regulations—but small steps will move us forward and lead to larger ones. This summer, we were able to get our annual powwow moved back to the ball field behind the old u.s.o. building, where it had been held in years past. Our next step will be to ask to have the Indian Museum given back to us. It was deeded to the town when my aunt Mabel died, but that was when we still controlled town hall. We're also going to try to do something about the restrictions that have been put on a fifty-eight-acre parcel of land we own down in South Mashpee, and we're looking into whatever became of the five-hundred-acre-parsonage woodlot that is supposed to go with our meetinghouse. The big thing, though, is for us to get federal recognition. That will provide us with health programs and education benefits, but most of all it will give us a sense of identity."

During a tour of South Mashpee, Vernon and I discussed what is far and away the most immediate threat to the Mashpee heritage he is determined to preserve—an extraordinarily rapid growth rate that is threatening to fill up the remaining open space in Mashpee and to pollute its drinking water. Between 1976 and 1979, land development in the town came to a virtual standstill because of the title threat presented by the first lawsuit. High interest rates also slowed growth, but once the appeals were turned down and interest rates fell, the floodgates opened. Since then, home- and condominium-building in Mashpee has proceeded at a fantastic pace, spurred by an all-white planning board whose members include several land developers. In 1983, a total of six hundred and thirty-four building permits were issued in Mashpee—three hundred and ninety-two of them for condominiums—and in the first eight months of 1984, six hundred and eighty-nine permits were issued, more than five hundred of them for condominiums. During that time, Mashpee issued more building permits than the entire township of Barnstable, which includes Hyannis—Cape Cod's largest town—and it issued more permits for condominiums than the Cape's fourteen other communities put together. Not surprisingly, this situation has finally begun to worry an appreciable segment of the town's non-Indian majority, including Mrs. Jean Thomas, a Mashpee selectman, who has described land development in Mashpee as a form of legal rape. As a result, the townspeople

recently voted to bring in a professional planner—a development that
Vernon Pocknett finds ironic, since it was unbridled land development
that led the Mashpees to bring their lawsuit in the first place.

Toward the end of our drive, Vernon and I turned off Waquoit
Road onto a dirt track that led a mile or so through some deep woods
to Punkhorn Point, a remote peninsula near the mouth of the Mashpee
River, where Vernon had beached his fishing boat to repair its hull.
A quarter of a mile or so across Popponesset Bay lay Daniel's Island,
where Earl Mills' father, Ferdinand, had found the tomahawk head
—it is now the site for a number of expensive summer homes—and
beyond the island was Popponesset Beach and Nantucket Sound. "My
father, Willard Pocknett, Jr., and I used to fish for oysters around
here," Vernon said. "He drowned over in Waquoit Bay after suffering
a heart attack and falling out of his boat. That was in 1948, when I
was only about fifteen years old, but he had already told me that one
day we would be fighting for the land in Mashpee. The first time he
told me was during the war, when we were staying down at our hunting
and fishing camp, just behind South Cape Beach. We got up one
morning and walked out on the beach, and saw a young fellow and a
girl, who were surfcasting. It was the first time we had ever seen
anyone on that beach who wasn't from Mashpee, and I can still remember what my father said. He said, 'Well, they're here, and that's
going to be the end of this place.' At the time, I couldn't believe he
meant it, but not long afterward, outsiders were able to acquire practically all of South Cape Beach. Then, during the early fifties, an outfit
called Field's Point Manufacturing Company, from Providence, came
in and dredged Popponesset Creek, filled in the marshland, pumped
sand up on the spits, built some summer cottages, and put in a marina.
A few years later, the New Seabury Corporation, which was formed
by some of the Field's Point people, acquired several thousand acres
in South Mashpee and built two sprawling golf courses, where we
used to hunt our deer, and God only knows how many fancy houses.
In no time at all, some of the people who bought into these new
communities decided to ignore the fact that we'd been around these
parts for several thousand years, and started running us off their beaches.
One day in the early nineteen-sixties, when I was bullraking oysters
from my boat on Popponesset Creek, a lady came out on her porch
and hollered at me to beat the band. 'Get out of here!' she yelled.
'And don't let me see your kind around here again!' I didn't say anything to her. I just kept bullraking away. I didn't need to say anything,

because I knew how long we'd been here, and I also knew we were going to be here a while longer."

Vernon's words took me back to the time I had visited Earl Mills in his apartment above The Flume, in 1978, just after the Mashpees had lost the first lawsuit. "What the lawsuit did was to bring out the real feelings of the whites," he had said softly. "It showed us the true depth of their hatred, their guilt, and their rage. We realize now that they would just as soon we disappeared off the face of the earth. Only, we aren't going to disappear." Mills had been braiding his daughter's hair. Now he patted her on the head, and watched her run out of the room. Then he turned to me and told me exactly the same thing his father had told me in the autumn of 1962. He said, "We're going to be here forever."

PART TWO

The Passamaquoddies and
the Penobscots

The Passamaquoddies and
the Penobscots

On a midweek afternoon in February of 1964, a Passamaquoddy Indian named George Stevens heard a chain saw start up in the woods next to his house, which sits on a narrow strip of land between Lewey's Lake and U.S. Route 1, in Indian Township, a Passamaquoddy reservation in the eastern part of Maine, a few miles from the New Brunswick border. Since Stevens knew that all Indian lands in the township were owned communally by the three hundred or so Passamaquoddies who lived there, and since he had not heard that any of them had been given permission by the Indian Township Tribal Council to cut wood in the lot adjacent to his house, he decided to investigate. After walking several hundred feet along the shoreline of the frozen lake, he came within sight of some tourist cabins owned by a white man named William Plaisted, and encountered a fellow Passamaquoddy wielding a chain saw, who explained that Plaisted had hired him to clear away the small growth on several acres of land that Plaisted had recently acquired next to the lake so that he could put in a road and build some additional cabins.

An hour later, Stevens walked out to Route 1 and flagged down his younger brother, John, who was driving home from his job, at the Georgia-Pacific Corporation paper mill in nearby Woodland, and told him what was happening. For several minutes, the two brothers stood by the side of the road discussing the situation and trying to decide what to do about it. John Stevens, the tribal governor at Indian Township, had been attempting to rally his people around the issue of land encroachment since 1957, when his wife's great-aunt, Louise Sockabesin, showed him a copy of a treaty made in 1794 between the Commonwealth of Massachusetts and the Passamaquoddy Tribe, which she had been keeping in a shoebox, and which, among other things, reserved for the Indians title in perpetuity to twenty-three thousand acres in the township and to fifteen islands in the St. Croix River and two islands in Big Lake, west of the township. Since none of the islands remained in Indian hands and only seventeen thousand of the original twenty-three thousand acres of land were listed as still being under Passamaquoddy ownership, it seemed to John Stevens that the treaty provided proof of a real-estate swindle of huge proportions, substantiating a complaint that the Passamaquoddies had been making for generations. Try as he might over the next five years, however, he was unable to find a single lawyer in Maine who was willing to take on a land-claim case in behalf of the Indians. Finally, he got discouraged and gave up. As for his fellow-Passamaquoddies, none of them seemed to know exactly how their lands had been alienated. Nor had any of them ever dared to protest the loss publicly, because, having been wards of the State of Maine for nearly a hundred and fifty years, they had become dependent on state handouts. During that time, the state had treated them in a manner that was sovereign, to say the least. It had sold much of their land outright; it had sold timber and grass rights on the remaining tracts to companies like Georgia-Pacific; and it had grossly mismanaged the meager tribal trust fund that had accrued from such transactions. By 1964, when the Stevens brothers held their conference on the shoulder of Route 1 — the road had been built through the reservation without the permission of its residents and without a penny of recompense paid to them and, indeed, had been paid for with the proceeds of nine-hundred-and-ninety-nine-year leases, which the state had granted on a mile-wide strip on either side of the road for its entire six-mile length — the Passamaquoddies at Indian Township had reached what was perhaps the lowest point in their history. Almost seventy-five percent of them were unemployed; a majority were on welfare; and many were suffering from alcoholism. As for their self-esteem, it was scarcely helped by the fact that most of their white neighbors looked upon them with scorn; indeed, as of 1964 no Passamaquoddy had ever been able to get a haircut in Princeton, the nearest town, just down the road from George Stevens' home.

The next night, John Stevens called a meeting of the Tribal Council in the parish hall at Peter Dana Point, an isolated Passamaquoddy settlement at Big Lake, four miles west of Route 1. News of Plaisted's intentions had spread rapidly through the Indian community, and the parish hall was packed. There was considerable talk at the meeting about how Plaisted had come to own property in Indian Township to begin with. It was recalled that he had been able to buy the land from the Town of Princeton just after the Second World War, when the state approved a transaction in which the town claimed possession of the land as payment for having incurred the funeral expenses of an indigent white man whom the Passamaquoddies had allowed to live on their reservation out of charity. In any event, although the Indians had long since accepted Plaisted as a neighbor and a landowner, resentment over what they considered the state's illegal approval of the affair was rekindled with a vengeance by word that Plaisted had acquired the latest piece of real estate in a poker game with another white man, who claimed that his title to it had also been validated by the state. This was the last straw as far as many of the Passamaquoddies were concerned, for none of them doubted that the land in question belonged to them. After further discussion, the Tribal Council voted to follow established procedure and request a meeting with the state attorney general, who, under the law, was supposed to represent the Indians in all disputes involving land. At the same time, the council, in order to show how seriously it viewed the matter, voted to seek an audience with Governor John Reed. Several weeks later, when the necessary arrangements had been made, the two Stevens brothers and their father, George, Sr., piled into an old station wagon with three other Passamaquoddies and drove two hundred miles to Augusta to keep a one o'clock appointment with the Governor.

For reasons that were never explained, Governor Reed kept the six men waiting in the anteroom of his office for five hours. When he finally consented to see the Indians, he told them that he had discussed the dispute with a number of politicians from the region around Indian Township, that he had been given to understand that interests other than Indian ones were involved, and that he could not intervene personally in the matter. He then referred the Passamaquoddies to the attorney general, who, after listening politely as they told him about the terms of the 1794 treaty, smiled and wished them well if they ever took their claim to court.

The six Passamaquoddies were bitterly disappointed by their treatment at the hands of the Governor and the attorney general. When they returned to Indian Township, they held another Tribal Council meeting in the parish hall and described to an overflow crowd how they had been received in Augusta. During the discussion that followed, a number of their fellow-tribesmen declared that the State of Maine was their enemy—something many of them had long felt but few had ever dared to say in public. Then the talk turned to strategy and tactics. At the end of the meeting, the Indians voted by a wide margin to block construction of the roadway into the disputed property and to prevent any new cabins from being built. They also decided that no firearms should be brought along and that there would be no violence. The prevailing mood in the parish hall was one of determination and pride tinged with anxiety and fear. No one present could remember when the Passamaquoddies had ever stood up to the whites in public.

The next morning, seventy-five Indians took up positions on Route 1, where some workers hired by Plaisted were preparing to lay a gravel road into the land he was claiming. When Plaisted, who lived in a house near his tourist cabins, came out to see what was going on, John Stevens informed him that the land belonged to the Passamaquoddy Tribe, and told him to leave the gravel, sand, and lumber that had been deposited upon it and not to proceed with any construction. Plaisted responded by asking for time to think things over— a request that Stevens granted—and went back into his house. An hour later, four state troopers and two game wardens arrived on the scene, along with a local policeman from Princeton. At lunchtime, John Stevens and most of the other Passamaquoddy demonstrators went home to eat, leaving five men (including George Stevens) and five women (including John's wife, Pauline) to continue the protest. The five men formed a line across the entrance to the proposed roadway, and the five women sat down on a large pile of sand that had been dumped beside it. Shortly thereafter, the men were taken into custody by the policeman from Princeton, who put them in his patrol car and drove to Woodland, where, informed by his "prisoners" that he had no jurisdiction to arrest them, he released them. By that time, however, the five women had been arrested by the state troopers and taken to Calais, twenty miles south, where they were charged with disorderly conduct and trespass and were locked up in the city jail. Later that afternoon, John Stevens went to Calais and obtained their release on bail for seventy-five dollars each. The next day, he drove over to Eastport and hired a lawyer named Don Gellers, who had recently arrived in town, to represent them.

Toward the end of April, when the case was brought before Judge John Dudley, of Maine District Court, in Calais, several hundred Indians were on hand, including a large contingent from the Passamaquoddy Reservation at Pleasant Point, some twenty miles to the southeast. When the case was called, Judge Dudley announced that

George and John Stevens at the site of the 1964 sit-in.
Photograph by Allen Sockabasin.

he had once served as Plaisted's attorney and had helped him acquire title to his land in Indian Township. On this basis, Gellers asked the Judge to disqualify himself. The request was granted, and the case was assigned to another judge. Before it could be tried, however, Gellers reached an agreement with the prosecutor that neither Plaisted nor the Passamaquoddies would set foot on the contested property until the question of who owned it had been setttled in court. The prosecutor then set aside the charges of trespass against the five Passamaquoddy women.

At that point, Gellers began to prepare a lawsuit aimed at restoring to the Indians the six thousand acres of land that had been alienated in violation of the 1794 treaty between the Commonwealth of Massachusetts and the Passamaquoddy Tribe. As it turned out, he was taking the first step in an astonishingly complex legal and political journey, which over the next decade would lead the members of the Passamaquoddy Tribe and the neighboring Penobscot Nation to the point where they would be able to lay valid legal claim to twelve and a half million acres of their aboriginal territory—an area that is nearly two-thirds of the state of Maine, and one inhabited by three hundred and fifty thousand whites.

Some anthropologists believe that the ancestors of the Indians arrived in Maine as early as eleven thousand years ago, after the Laurentide Icecap had receded, and they point to carvings on shell pendants found in subsequent burial sites to suggest that these prehistoric explorers shared a vast expanse of inhospitable tundra with the great woolly mammoth. Year-round occupation of the region probably did not begin, however, until forests suitable for hunting game and gathering food had grown up—a process generally estimated to have taken six millennia. Indian burial sites dating back five thousand years indicate that the residents of Maine at that time were part of a widespread culture of Algonquian-speaking people who hunted with spears and travelled in dugout canoes. Much later, after developing the bow and arrow and the use of birch bark, the Indians of Maine and the Maritime Provinces formed the Wabanaki Confederacy (the name "Wabanaki" means "people of the dawn"), which included the Micmacs, the Malecites, the Passamaquoddies, and the Penobscots. Each of these tribes possessed a definite territory, usually along one of the large rivers flowing into the Atlantic. Thereafter, using the river as a highway and its banks as vegetable gardens, the Indians migrated with the seasons between forested interior and the seacoast, planting and harvesting corn, squash, and beans; hunting moose and caribou; trapping beaver, otter, and muskrat; catching eels, seals, and porpoises; fishing for alewives, bass, shad, and salmon; and gathering clams and lobsters.

When the Europeans first arrived in North America, the Passamaquoddies were living on the shores of Passamaquoddy Bay, near the mouth of the St. Croix River. (According to some scholars, the name "Passamaquoddy" means "place of the undertow people," and refers to the phenomenal tidal fall in that region, which can be as much as twenty feet.) Because the Passamaquoddies were coastal dwellers, they may have come in contact with the Italian navigator Giovanni da Verrazano, who sailed up the coast from what later became known as Cape Fear, North Carolina, to Newfoundland in 1524 in search of a northwest passage to India. Their first extended encounter with whites did not take place until the winter of 1604–5, however, when Samuel de Champlain and the Huguenot leader Pierre du Guast, Sieur de Monts, built a fort on Dochet Island, in the St. Croix River. Before abandoning the settlement the following spring, the Frenchmen forged strong ties with the local residents, whom Champlain's chronicler described as having "courage, fidelity, generosity, humanity, and hospitality, judgment, and good sense." In addition to these fine character traits, the Indians at Passamaquoddy had luck, for they inhabited a remote area that, as it turned out, remained beyond the reach of English settlers for the next hundred and fifty years.

Their colleagues elsewhere in Maine were not so fortunate. The tribes to the west of Penobscot River, their numbers reduced by plague and savage encounters with the Mohawks, began giving way to colonists from Massachusetts, who established fishing and trading posts along the coast. Then, in 1675, the Indian uprising called King Philip's War broke out in southern New England, and a long period of sporadic hostilities between the Indians and the settlers began in the part of Massachusetts that eventually became Maine. By that time, some six thousand whites were living there, mostly in the coastal region between Kittery and Monhegan Island, and during the next eighty-five years—a period marked by six separate conflicts—more than a thousand of them were killed by Indians. By the end of the French and Indian Wars, in 1763, the tribes living west of the Penobscot had been vanquished, and after the Treaty of Paris, when France ceded Canada to England, the Indians who remained on the frontier had to deal with the victors from Massachusetts as best they could. A few years earlier, Massachusetts had taken possession of that portion of the Penobscot Nation's territory which lay below the head of the tide at the falls in the river near the present city of Bangor. However, in official correspondence with leaders of the Penobscot Nation, Massachusetts acknowledged the right of the Penobscots to continue to occupy and use all the territory above the head of the tide.

For the next dozen years, Massachusetts respected its word, and, needing allies for the approaching Revolution, was even solicitous of the Indians' territorial prerogatives. In 1775, the Massachusetts Provincial Congress enacted a resolve forbidding trespass on lands adjacent to the Penobscot River which were "now claimed by our brethren the Indians of the Penobscot Tribe," and pledged that the inhabitants of the colony would "distain to make use of unjustifiable force or artifice to rob their unsuspecting brethren of their rights." And the Passamaquoddies were now seen as occupying strategic territory on the Canadian border. In 1776, they received a chain of friendship from General George Washington, and a year later they pledged their support to the American colonies when John Allan, the Continental Congress's representative to the Eastern Indians, promised that their hunting grounds would be safeguarded and that they would be "forever viewed as brothers and children under the Protection and Fatherly care of the United States."

By all accounts, the Indians acquitted themselves admirably during the Revolutionary War, and were generally credited with saving Eastern Maine for the colonies. The Passamaquoddies, for example, were instrumental in turning back a British naval expedition that attacked Machias in August of 1777. In the engagement, Francis Joseph Neptune, who later became chief of the Passamaquoddy Tribe, fired a musket shot from an incredible distance, killing the commander of the lead British vessel. The exploits of the Passamaquoddies prompted Allan, who was also a colonel in the Massachusetts militia, to declare that "no people will defend the liberty of America better." After the war, Allan reminded the Continental Congress of the contributions that the Passamaquoddies had made to the revolutionary cause, and urged that the promises he had given them on the government's behalf be fulfilled. Congress did not act on his recommendations, however, and soon revoked his appointment. Allan subsequently became a commissioner for the Commonwealth of Massachusetts, and in 1794 he

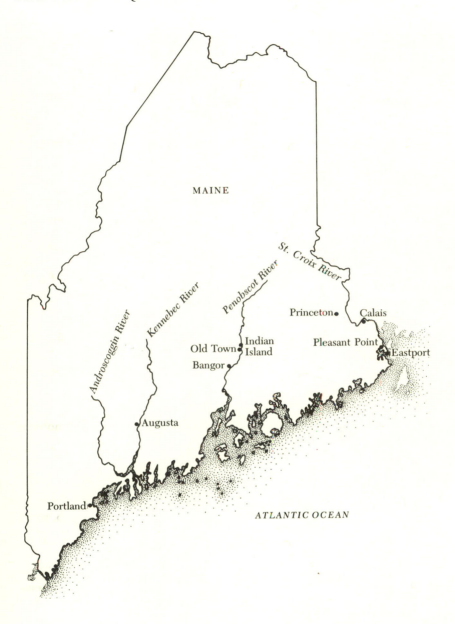

Map of Maine, showing the Penobscot Reservation on Indian Island in the Penobscot River just north of Old Town, and the Passamaquoddy reservations at Lewey's Lake, in Princeton, and at Pleasant Point.

helped negotiate the treaty that Louise Sockabesin later showed to John Stevens. Under its provisions, the Passamaquoddies relinquished all claims to lands within Massachusetts except for the twenty-three-thousand-acre township, the islands in the St. Croix River and Big Lake, a ten-acre tract of land at Pleasant Point (which the Commonwealth later increased to a hundred acres), and the right to fish in both branches of the St. Croix River.

Meanwhile, the Penobscots had come under strong pressure from Massachusetts to surrender their claim to a vast territory in the watershed of the river for which they were named, and in 1796 they were finally persuaded to give up nearly two hundred thousand acres in exchange for a hundred and fifty yards of blue cloth for blankets, four hundred pounds of shot, a hundred pounds of powder, a hundred bushels of corn, thirteen bushels of salt, thirty-six hats, a barrel of rum, and the promise of an annual stipend consisting of similar items. From then on, their days as property owners of consequence were numbered. In 1818, impoverished and desperately in need of additional provisions, they ceded to Massachusetts all their remaining lands except the islands in the Penobscot River above Old Town, about twelve miles north of Bangor, and four six-mile-square townships from which they hoped to sell timber and make their living. The final big grab occurred in 1833, when the State of Maine—which had separated from the Union in 1820—bought the four townships for fifty thousand dollars in a fraudulent transaction involving forged signatures.

Once the three hundred or so Penobscots who remained had been deprived of their patrimony, they found themselves consigned to a tiny ghetto community on Indian Island, just above the Penobscot River at Old Town. As for the Passamaquoddies, who numbered about four hundred, by 1850 they were reduced to living in two isolated settlements—one on the Atlantic coast at Pleasant Point, a barren promontory bounded on three sides by the waters of Passamaquoddy and Cobscook Bays, and the other at Peter Dana Point, a remote peninsula dividing Big Lake and Long Lake, in Indian Township, some fifty miles away. As far as their white neighbors were concerned, the Indians were now expected to become extinct—"gradually diminishing," one observer predicted, "as other tribes, once their powerful neighbors, have done before them, till there shall be none remaining." In the years that followed, however, the Penobscots and the Passamaquoddies intermarried extensively, increased in numbers, and, in spite of poverty, oppression, and a lack of adequate education, managed to retain a strong sense of their Indian identity. They also became convinced that they had lost their lands unfairly. This conviction grew stronger after the Second World War, and so did their frustration when they saw blacks and other minority groups asserting their rights and redressing grievances elsewhere in the United States. When they finally came to realize that they were virtually powerless, some form of protest was inevitable. For the Pasamaquoddies, its culmination was the sit-in on the pile of sand at Plaisted's.

During the summer that followed the sit-in, a young man from St. Louis named Thomas Tureen, who had just finished his sophomore year at Princeton, got a job as a physical-eduation instructor at a school in Pierre, South Dakota, that was run by the United States Interior Department's Bureau of Indian Affairs. Tureen could scarcely believe his eyes when he arrived at his new post. The two hundred students at the school, who were mostly Sioux, had been removed from their homes on reservations in South Dakota and Montana, and were not being allowed to return for summer vacation, because of what the government deemed to be adverse family situations. Moreover, while they were at the school they not only were not allowed to speak any Indian language but were punished if they did. One of Tureen's fellow-instructors actually carried a club on his belt to enforce this prohibition and maintain discipline. By the end of the summer, Tureen had become convinced that the boarding school was, in essence, an internment camp, and that the young Indians there were essentially captives. The experience changed his life. He had intended to major in literature and poetry. Now, appalled and fascinated by the relationship that existed between the Indians and the federal government, which exercised almost complete control over their lives, he became interested in law.

After graduating from Princeton, Tureen entered law school at George Washington University, in Washington, D.C., and went to work part time for Edgar Cahn's Citizens' Advocate Center, where he helped do research for a book highly critical of the Bureau of Indian Affairs. (It was published in 1969, under the title "Our Brother's Keeper: The Indian in White America.") He also signed up to work with the Law Students' Civil Rights Research Council, a national organization that provides law-student clerks to lawyers engaged in civil rights work. In the spring of 1967, because he had fallen in love

Joseph Attien, last hereditary chief of the Penobscot Nation, first elected governor of the tribe, and guide of Thoreau. Photograph of a tintype made around 1862, when Attien was about 33 years old. Courtesy of the Fannie Hardy Eckstorm Collection, Folger Library, University of Maine at Orono.

with a senior at Sarah Lawrence named Susan Albright (she later became his wife), and hoped to be near her during the summer vacation, he told the council that he wanted to work on Indian cases in the East. As it happened, the council had received only one request for a clerk that met this requirement. It had come from Don Gellers, in Eastport.

By that time, Gellers had put together a detailed account of how the Passamaquoddies lost six thousand acres of the original twenty-three thousand acres of land that had been reserved to them under the 1794 treaty, and he had begun to explore ways in which he might be able to bring about its restitution. During the summer that Tureen clerked for him, Gellers was working on the theory that Maine had violated the provisions of the 1794 treaty between Massachusetts and his clients. One problem with this approach was that Maine was one of the few remaining states in the Union that had refused to waive sovereign immunity; this meant that it could not be sued by anyone other than the United States or another state without its consent. To get around this obstacle, Gellers decided to sue Massachusetts, which had waived sovereign immunity, the ground for the suit being that the Passamaquoddies had never released Massachusetts from its obligations under the 1794 treaty. The idea behind this strategy was that Massachusetts would then be forced to sue Maine. Because Gellers wanted an attorney familiar with Massachusetts law, he obtained the services of John S. Bottomly, a lawyer practicing in Boston, who had achieved public notice when he was put in charge of the investigation of the Boston Strangler murder case by the state's attorney general. (In the film that was made about the case, the role of Bottomly was played by Henry Fonda.) On March 8, 1968, Gellers and Bottomly began a suit against Massachusetts in behalf of the Passamaquoddy Tribe for a hundred and fifty million dollars as compensation for past mismanagement of its tribal trust fund. Three days later, Gellers was arrested by a Maine narcotics agent at his home in Eastport and charged with possession of marijuana. During the months that followed, he became almost wholly preoccupied with defending himself against this charge. As a result, Joint Tribal Council of the Passamaquoddy Tribe v. the Commonwealth of Masachusetts was never argued in Suffolk Superior Court in Boston, and the Passamaquoddies were once again without a lawyer.

This state of affairs continued until June of 1969, when Tureen finished law school. At that point, encouraged by John Stevens, with whom he had become friendly two summers before, he returned to Maine, opened an office in Calais, and went to work for the Indian Legal Services Unit of Pine Tree Legal Assistance—a statewide program financed by the Office of Economic Opportunity to provide lawyers for poor people involved in civil cases. For the remainder of the year, Tureen represented Passamaquoddy clients in proceedings involving divorces, bill collections, and petty disputes. Then, in the winter of 1970, he began helping the tribe set up organizations and corporations that would enable it to receive grants from various federal agencies. This led him to wonder why the Passamaquoddies had never received any financial assistance from the Bureau of Indian Affairs, which, as he knew from his research for "Our Brother's Keeper," was the lead agency for such aid. Upon looking further into the matter, Tureen found that B.I.A. money went only to those tribes whose land was held in trust by the United States or was held subject to a federal restriction against alienation, and that federal money was almost never allocated to the tribes living in states that evolved from the original thirteen colonies. He then undertook to study the basic statute for that restriction—the Indian Nonintercourse Act of 1790, which was passed by the First Congress to protect the Indians from land grabbers, and which prohibits the sale of Indian lands without the express approval of Congress.

The more Tureen pondered the language of the Nonintercourse Act, the more he became convinced that it ought to apply to the Passamaquoddies, in spite of the fact that states that had evolved from the thirteen original colonies had never accepted the statute as limiting their power over Indian tribes living within their borders. With Francis O'Toole, a student at the University of Maine School of Law and editor-in-chief of the school's *Law Review*, who had been working on Indian law for several years, he now undertook to examine the legal and legislative premises lying behind the sweeping jurisdiction that Maine had long exercised over its Indians. After several months of exhaustive research, the two men concluded that there was no basis whatever for the commonly held assumption that the Nonintercourse Act did not apply to tribes living in what had been the thirteen original colonies. Nor could they find any evidence that the treaty of 1794 with Massachusetts had been made in compliance with the Nonintercourse Act or had ever been approved by Congress. In an article published in the *Maine Law Review* in the spring of 1971, Tureen and O'Toole outlined their findings in considerable detail and leveled a harsh indictment of the federal government's policy toward the Indians in Maine. "The Department of Interior has failed to fulfill the national guardianship duty owed to Maine's tribes," they wrote. "Some of the blame must lie with the United States Congress, which has failed to exercise the power vested in it by the United States Constitution. The failure of the Department of Interior to fulfill its duty and of Congress to exercise its power, however, has created no rights in the State of Maine. The federal government has never surrendered its power over Maine's tribes. That power must be resurrected and the many wrongs must be remedied."

At the time, neither Tureen's colleagues in the legal profession nor, for that matter, anyone at all in a position of power and responsibility in Maine paid much attention to the article. The Passamaquoddy Tribal Council, however, fired Gellers, who had been convicted of one of the charges against him—"constructive" possession of marijuana—and sentenced to a term in prison, and asked Tureen to take over the land-claim case. He willingly accepted. In the winter of 1980, during the first of several visits I paid him at his office in Portland, Tureen—a short, energetic man with a shrewd mind, a self-confident manner, and an impish smile—told me, "I knew as early as 1970 that the Passamaquoddy land claim could lead to an incredibly big lawsuit. I remember coming home very excited one night and telling my wife that if what I had figured out about the Nonintercourse Act was correct the Passamaquoddies could lay claim to a million acres. Later, when I had actually been given the case to handle, it struck me that, with so much real estate at stake, I was bound to come up against some pretty heavy going, and that a case this big would require the efforts of a legal team. I also realized from observing the Gellers affair that an individual attorney is comparatively easy to pick off. I had spent enough time on Capitol Hill to learn how easily political pressure can be brought to bear on government agencies, and the fact that Pine Tree Legal Assistance was financed by O.E.O. made me kind of uneasy. For these reasons, one of the first things I did was go out and line up some independent legal and financial backing."

In the spring of 1971, Tureen persuaded the Native American Rights Fund to act as co-counsel. "Later on, I went to work for NARF full time, on salary," he said. "There was never any question of my handling the Passamaquoddy case on a contingency fee. In addition to enlisting the aid of NARF, I went shopping for a large law firm to participate pro bono. First, I visited Arthur Lazarus, Jr., in the Washington office of Fried, Frank, Harris, Shriver & Kampelman. He had handled cases under the Indian Claims Commission Act—a 1946 law that, among other things, allowed Indians whose land had been taken unfairly to sue the United States for an amount equal to the value of the land at the time it was taken—and I had heard that he was very knowledgeable about Indian affairs. Incidentally, for the past twenty-four years Lazarus has been one of the attorneys for the Sioux Nation of Indians in its battle to win compensation for the government's acquisition of the Black Hills portion of the Sioux Reservation back in 1877, and he recently helped win an award of nearly a hundred and six million dollars for his clients, which is the largest award ever made under the Indian Claims Commission Act. In 1971, however, when I told him that the Passamaquoddy Tribe had a million-acre claim dating back to 1794, he sat quietly in his chair and did some figuring in his head. As I recall our conversation, he then told me that such a claim would amount to only about three hundred thousand dollars, and that the case would not warrant the time and money required to litigate it. I said, 'Mr. Lazarus, this is not an Indian Claims Commission case, this is a Nonintercourse Act claim.' At that, he shook his head and told me I was dreaming. Afterward, I went to the firm of Hogan & Hartson, which had a separate division set up to do free work for deserving clients, and the people there came on board with enthusiasm. Finally, I was lucky enough to get Barry Margolin, a brilliant young law student at Northeastern University, in Boston, who would later handle the Mashpee land-claim case, and David Crosby, who had been editor-in-chief of the University of Southern California *Law Review* and was then an attorney with California Indian Legal Services, to come up to Calais and work on the case full time. I now had a team of first-rate attorneys, including Robert Pelcyger, of NARF, Robert Mittel, of Pine Tree Legal Assistance, and Stuart Ross, of Hogan & Hartson, to help me, and I was hoping that the give-and-take among us would produce a first-rate piece of litigation. One thing was certain—the Passamaquoddy claim was so big we sure as hell weren't going to win on sympathy."

The chief problem that now confronted Tureen and his colleagues was how to convert into a legal reality the theory that the provisions of the Nonintercourse Act applied to the Passamaquoddy Tribe, and that the tribe was therefore entitled to the return of its entire aboriginal territory, and the special services that the federal government gives to Indians, and the special governmental status that American Indian tribes enjoy. "We had to figure out a way to get this huge claim into court," Tureen said. "To begin with, we knew we were going to have to find a way around the problem of sovereign immunity. Gellers' plan—to bring suit against Massachusetts in the hope that Massachusetts would be forced to sue Maine—was unacceptable. For one thing, it depended on state courts, which we were afraid might be prejudiced against the Indians. For another, it rested on the assumption that the treaty made in 1794 between the Commonwealth of Massachusetts and the Passamaquoddy Tribe was valid, and thus gave away everything except the claim for the six thousand acres that had been taken from Indian Township during the years that followed. It also meant abandoning any hope of obtaining federal services or governmental status. We decided that a much better way would be to bring an action in federal court against the State of Maine and its landowners for the entire million-acre claim, on the ground that the 1794 treaty violated the federal Indian Nonintercourse Act. We would still have to deal with sovereign immunity, however, because the Eleventh Amendment to the Constitution prohibits a private party from suing a state in federal court. Happily, our research turned up an obscure case that promised a way out of this dilemma. It was brought by George Lee, a son of General Robert E. Lee and his wife, Mary, and it involved land that had been taken from Mary Lee without due process and without compensation during the Civil War and turned into Arlington National Cemetery. In 1882, the Supreme Court ruled that George Lee, who had inherited the land from his mother, could bring suit in federal court for return of the land, the Eleventh Amendment notwithstanding, on the ground that since the property had been taken in violation of the Constitution, it was in the possession of those agents of the government who were illegally occupying it, and not in the possession of the government itself, for the simple reason that the government could not violate its own laws. On the basis of this case alone, we hoped that the Passamaquoddy Tribe would be able to sue Maine in federal court for having violated the Nonintercourse Act. However, we would then have to get around a second problem, which involved a legal doctrine known as the well-pleaded-complaint rule. You see, federal courts generally have the power to hear only actions between citizens of different states, or actions that arise under federal law. Since the Passamaquoddy Tribe was a resident of Maine, it was obvious that we could not get into federal court against the State of Maine on the basis of diversity of citizenship. Thus, our only hope of invoking federal-court jurisdiction was to claim that our proposed law-suit was based on a violation of the federal Nonintercourse Act. The trouble here was an earlier Supreme Court ruling that an action could be construed to arise under federal law only if the federal-law issue appeared in a complaint that contained nothing superfluous—a decision that had come to be known as the well-pleaded-complaint rule. Since the Passamaquoddies were seeking possession of land and monetary damages for trespass, they would be filing a simple ejectment action, which, if it were to be considered well pleaded, should state nothing more than that the Indians were entitled to possession of the land, and that the State of Maine was keeping them out.

"We soon discovered that our fears about the well-pleaded-complaint rule were far from theoretical, for, as it happened, an extremely important land claim brought by the Oneida Indian Nation against the County of Oneida in New York State had just been rejected in District Court, on this very ground. In attempting to establish their right to have their case heard in federal court, the Oneidas had included in their ejectment complaint an allegation that they were entitled to possession of certain parcels of land because of the Nonintercourse Act. The court, however, found that this allegation was superfluous, and dismissed the action on the basis of the well-pleaded-complaint rule. As things turned out, the Supreme Court would reverse this ruling in 1974, on the ground that federal regulation of all Indian lands is so pervasive that there cannot be a dispute involving Indian land which does not, in turn, involve federal law. But the Supreme Court reversal was three years down the road, of course, and in 1971 the well-pleaded-complaint rule caused us a lot of worry."

Tureen went on to say that in addition to the problems posed by the Eleventh Amendment and the well-pleaded-complaint rule, he and his colleagues faced the prospect of having to deal with various time-related defenses, such as laches, adverse possession, and statutes of limitation. " 'Laches' simply means that you have sat on your hands too long," he explained, "and 'adverse possession' is just another way of saying 'squatters' rights.' However, our research had revealed that no time-related defense based on state law could defeat an Indian claim filed by the federal government under the Nonintercourse Act, and we thought that the same exemption might apply to an Indian tribe filing a claim on its own. Only a federal statute of limitations could clearly defeat this kind of claim. We had never heard of such a statute, but just to make doubly certain we decided to go looking. When we did, we found to our shock and surprise that on July 18, 1966, Congress had adopted a statute of limitations which declared that all claims for monetary damages for wrongful use of Indian land brought on behalf of any Indians by the United States government would have to be filed within six years of the time the wrong occurred, and that for purposes of the statute old claims such as those of the Passamaquoddy Tribe were deemed to have accrued on the date of passage. This meant that if we couldn't persuade the government to bring legal action in behalf of the Passamaquoddy Tribe before July 18, 1972—then just eight months away—we would have to risk filing the claim for damages for a hundred and eighty years of trespass, potentially worth billions of dollars, on our own. While we had theories as to why the Eleventh Amendment, the well-pleaded-complaint rule, and the state-law time defenses should not defeat a Nonintercourse Act claim brought by the tribe in federal court, the trouble was that they were just theories. On the other hand, it had been clearly established that none of these defenses could stop a Nonintercourse Act claim brought by the United State in behalf of a tribe. That was the clincher as far as strategy was concerned. Somehow or other, we were going to have to find a way to get the feds to sue the state."

In December of 1971, Tureen appeared before the members of the Joint Tribal Council of the Passamaquoddy Tribe, meeting in the parish hall at Peter Dana Point, and told them that the 1794 treaty with Massachusetts was null and void, because it had never been approved by Congress. He explained that as a result the Passamaquoddy Tribe could now bring suit not just for the six thousand acres that had been purloined from its holdings at Indian Township but for its entire ancestral hunting grounds—an immense area of more than a million acres, lying between the Narraguagus and St. Croix Rivers. After outlining the various legal options, he recommended that the Tribal Council ask the federal government to initiate such an action on its behalf. There were a few moments of astonished silence. Then, after taking a unanimous vote, the council decided to go ahead.

On February 22, 1972—Washington's Birthday—the governor of the Passamaquoddy Tribe at Indian Township and the governor at Pleasant Point jointly wrote a letter to Louis R. Bruce, the Commissioner of the Bureau of Indian Affairs, in Washington, D.C. After

reminding Bruce of the promises that had been made to the Passamaquoddy Tribe by Washington, and of the services that the Passamaquoddies had rendered to the revolutionary cause, the two governors
cited some of the evidence gathered by Tureen to show that the lands
of the tribe should have been protected by the federal government
under the Nonintercourse Act. They also requested that Bruce ask
the Department of Justice to initiate a lawsuit against Maine for the
return of the land and for monetary damages, and to do so before the
July 18 deadline imposed by the statute of limitations.

"Writing the letter on Washington's Birthday was, of course, a
symbolic gesture," Tureen told me. "In any event, Louis Bruce, a
Mohawk from New York State, became convinced that the Passamaquoddy claim had merit, and early in March he sent a memo recommending approval of the governors' request on up through channels
in the Interior Department. Several weeks passed, and when April
came we still had no reply. But that time, however, we had learned
that the memo had reached the desk of William Gershuny, the Associate Solicitor for Indian Affairs, who was the top legal officer in the
department for Indian matters. Gershuny was not known to have any
special sympathy for Indians, but I went down to Washington to see
him, in the hope that I could persuade him to take some action. I was
only twenty-eight at the time, and I guess I was still fairly naïve. At
our meeting, Gershuny told me that the whole business was very
complicated and his division would need more time to study it, so I
thanked him and came back to Calais. April went by, May arrived,
and, with the July deadline fast approaching, we began firing off des-
perate telegrams to Gershuny, who responded by telling us that the
matter was still under advisement. By then, it was becoming clear
that we were being stalled, so in mid-May I went to Augusta and paid
a call on Governor Kenneth Curtis"—he had succeeded John Reed
in 1967—"and told him about the situation. The governor couldn't
have been more sympathetic. He issued a public statement saying
that if the Passamaquoddies had a valid claim they should have their
day in court, like all other Americans, and that a case of this importance
should not be allowed to go by default by letting the statute of limitations run out."

The very next day, Tureen flew to Washington and elicited similar expressions of support from Senator Margaret Chase Smith, Senator Edmund S. Muskie, and Maine's two representatives—William
Hathaway and Peter Kyros. Senator Smith was especially helpful. She

wrote a letter to Interior Secretary Rogers C. B. Morton urging him to take quick action on the Passamaquoddies' petition. She also called the White House, and Bradley Patterson, President Nixon's staff man for Indian affairs then called Gershuny. "When we heard about the details of that conversation between Patterson and Gershuny, we knew for sure that Interior was leading us up the garden path," Tureen said. "An attorney friend of mine quoted Gershuny as saying that it was high time the Indians accepted the facts of life. Gershuny also pointed out to the White House that the statute of limitations was about to expire, and that no court had ever ordered the federal government to file a lawsuit on behalf of anyone, much less a multi-million-dollar lawsuit on behalf of a powerless and virtually penniless Indian tribe. At this point, we realized that Gershuny was a step ahead of us. He was assuming that any attempt on our part to obtain a court order forcing the government to act on behalf of the Passamaquoddies would fail, because of a time-honored legal doctrine called prosecutorial discretion. Now, there was no question in our mind that this doctrine could spell bad trouble for us, and that we would have to find a way around it. Federal judges hate to get involved with the actual running of government, you see, and they especially dislike second-guessing purely discretionary decisions, such as those a government lawyer must make in deciding whether or not to prosecute a lawsuit. In fact, although federal judges routinely correct administrative decision-makers who act on the basis of an incorrect understanding of the law, no federal judge in the entire history of American jurisprudence had ever ordered the government to file a lawsuit. Unfortunately, it was just such an order that we desperately needed."

As Tureen and his colleagues pondered the problem of prosecutorial discretion, they became increasingly nervous, for it was now the middle of May, and the statute of limitations was due to expire in two months. "Although the language of the statute spoke only of claims filed by the government for money damages, we feared that it might be broadly construed by a court to include actions for possession of land, whether they be brought by the government or a tribe," Tureen said. "In short, we faced the prospect of the entire Passamaquoddy claim becoming moot if we were not able to force the government to file before July 18th. Then, all of a sudden, Stuart Ross came up with the idea that the very threat of mootness might provide a way out of our quandary. He reminded us that Article III, Section Two, of the Constitution provides that judges have power to adjudicate only live controversies, as opposed to moot or academic questions of law, but he also pointed out that under the common law judges have practically unlimited power to preserve an issue once it is properly before the court. Thus, if we could convince the court that there was a valid dispute between the Passamaquoddy Tribe and the Interior Department over the meaning of the Nonintercourse Act, and further convince the court that it was going to lose its jurisdiction to adjudicate this issue when the statute of limitations ran out, we might be able to persuade the court to order the government to file suit in behalf of the tribe in order to preserve its jurisdiction to decide the question of the applicability of the Nonintercourse Act to the Maine Indians. Since the court would technically be ordering the government to do no more than merely file the suit—in order to forestall the running of the statute of limitations—it would not be interfering with the doctrine of prosecutorial discretion. And while such an order would not guarantee that the government would eventually proceed with the claim, the filing of it was bound to provide a powerful impetus to do so, and would be an immensely important strategic victory. After considering the various pros and cons of the matter, we decided to use the common law enabling judges to preserve their jurisdiction in a last-ditch effort to unlock the door that the people at Interior had shut in our faces. It was a gamble, of course, but with the statute of limitations running out on us, what else could we do?"

On June 2, 1972, Tureen and his colleagues filed suit on behalf of the Passamaquoddies against Secretary Morton and other government officials in the federal district court in Portland, seeking a declaratory judgment that the tribe was entitled to the protection of the Nonintercourse Act, and requesting a preliminary injunction ordering the defendants to file a protective action for monetary damages against the State of Maine before the statute of limitations expired. Two weeks later, United States District Court Judge Edward T. Gignoux, a jurist of widely acknowledged excellence, who had been appointed by President Eisenhower in 1957, held the first of two lengthy hearings on Passamaquoddy v. Morton, and Tureen found himself arguing in federal court for the first time in his career. "I was terribly nervous," he recalled. "So were my colleagues, Stuart Ross and Barry Margolin. After all, we were going for broke in a make-or-break situation. I began by pointing out to Judge Gignoux that under the provisions of the Administrative Procedure Act an unreasonable delay was deemed to be a denial of a request. Then I told him that we believed that

United States District Court Judge Edward T. Gignoux.
Courtesy of Associated Press/Wide World Photos.

officials of the Interior Department had unreasonably delayed and thus, under the Administrative Procedure Act, technically denied the Passamaquoddies' request. I said that we believed that the government had done this because it had assumed incorrectly that the Nonintercourse Act did not apply to Indians living in states that had evolved from the thirteen original colonies. Finally, I asked him to order the government to file a protective action on behalf of the tribe, not for the benefit of the tribe but as a means of protecting the court's jurisdiction to hear the case involving the question of whether or not the Nonintercourse Act did in fact apply to the Passamaquoddy Tribe. It was a highly unusual request, because it broke new legal ground, and Judge Gignoux was clearly reluctant to issue the momentous order that would grant it unless he had to. He was undoubtedly hoping that the government would also want to avoid such a precedent, and would voluntarily file a protective suit in behalf of the tribe. However, it soon became apparent that Dennis Wittman, the lawyer from the Justice Department who was representing the federal defendants, had no authority to take this step. As a result, Judge Gignoux concluded the first hearing by ordering the government to report to him within a week on whether it would voluntarily file suit on behalf of the tribe, and, if the decision was negative, to state its reasons.

In a show-cause hearing held on June 23rd, Wittman conceded that the Nonintercourse Act applied in the states that had evolved from the thirteen original colonies, but he informed Judge Gignoux that the government would not sue the State of Maine on behalf of the Passamaquoddy Tribe, because the act applied only to tribes that had been granted federal recognition. In doing so, Wittman made a serious error. In order to scotch our claim, he need only have told Judge Gignoux that the government was refusing to act on the tribe's request because the case was weak, or because filing the action would have been inconsistent with government policy. Instead, he substituted one legal argument for another—the allegation that the Nonintercourse Act did not apply to nonrecognized tribes, as opposed to the contention that the Act applied only outside the original thirteen states—and thus confirmed that there was indeed a real controversy between the Passamaquoddies and the federal government, which Judge Gignoux had the power to adjudicate, and which would soon become moot if no lawsuit were filed on behalf of the tribe. Judge Gignoux was obviously disappointed by Wittman's response, and he pressed Wittman to explain the government's position further. Wittman replied that ordering the United States Attorney General to file such a lawsuit might do serious damage to relations between the federal government and the State of Maine. Judge Gignoux then observed that the governor of Maine and the state's entire congressional delegation had called for the action to be brought. At that point, the United States Attorney for Maine, Peter Mills, who had been sitting at the counsel table next to Wittman, jumped to his feet and declared that he, too, wanted the government to bring suit. With that, everybody in the courtroom broke out laughing, and shortly thereafter Judge Gignoux called for a recess. When he came back, a while later, he ordered the Department of Justice to file the protective action."

Late in June, the Justice Department complied with Judge Gignoux's order by filing a hundred-and-fifty-million-dollar damage suit against the State of Maine on behalf of the Passamaquoddy Tribe. Two weeks later—one day before the statute of limitations was due to expire—the Department filed suit for the same amount in behalf of the Penobscot Nation. "In April, Francis Ranco, governor of the Penobscot Nation, had invited me to meet with the Penobscot Tribal Council at Indian Island, in Old Town," Tureen told me. "The members of the council had heard about the letter the Passamaquoddies sent to Louis Bruce at the Bureau of Indian Affairs, and they wanted to know if I thought they should also take steps to initiate a land claim. However, they were by no means persuaded that it was a good course to pursue. The turning point of the meeting came when one of the more skeptical members of the council asked me what I really thought the Penobscots could hope to get out of such a farfetched lawsuit. I replied that if everything worked perfectly the tribe might be in a position to negotiate a settlement within five years, and that a negotiated settlement could be realistically expected to bring each tribe as much as two hundred thousand acres of land, ten million dollars, federal recognition, and various federal immunities that they did not then enjoy. Some of the council members thought I was dreaming, while others worried that involvement with the feds would lead to federal control of their land. In the end, however, they authorized Governor Ranco to send Commissioner Bruce the same kind of letter the Passamaquoddies had sent him in February. After Judge Gignoux ruled in favor of the Passamaquoddies, the Justice Department saw the handwriting on the wall and agreed to file a protective action for the Penobscots. A few hours before the statute was to expire, Congress extended it for ninety days, and that turned out to be the first of many extensions. We had been seeking the extension in case the court action did not work, so when both came through we began to wonder if all the anxiety and tension of the spring had been for nothing. In retrospect, however, we realized that the statute had been a blessing in disguise. True, it had placed us under terrible pressure, but it had also been the crucial factor in influencing Judge Gignoux to order the protective action. After all, the Judge could hardly have failed to see that the Passamaquoddy Tribe would suffer irreparable damage if the courts were to decide after the statute ran out that the Indians had been entitled to federal protection all along."

Once the protective suits had been filed, Judge Gignoux ordered them held in abeyance pending the outcome of Passamaquoddy v. Morton, and in the winter of 1973, after an appeal of his earlier decision had been dismissed by the Court of Appeals for the First Circuit, he turned his attention to the Nonintercourse Act issue. What was at issue in Passamaquoddy v. Morton was perfectly straightforward. On the one hand, the plaintiffs claimed that the Nonintercourse Act applied to the Passamaquoddy Tribe and that it established a trust relationship between the United States and the Indians. On the other hand, the defendants—they now included Maine, which intervened as a party defendant—contended that the act did not apply to the Passamaquoddy Tribe, because the tribe had never been officially recognized by the federal government. The defendants also claimed that no trust relationship existed.

What was at stake was simply mind-boggling, of course, for if the case should be decided in favor of the Passamaquoddies the central issue in suits involving billions of dollars and a staggering amount of real estate would be resolved. With the protective suits in abeyance, however, the potential consequences of Passamaquoddy v. Morton remained out of public sight and mind. According to Tureen, it was not uncommon in those days to hear people in Maine saying that the Indians should be given a fair shake. "What was uncommon was to hear anybody raise the possibility that this might result in a sizable chunk of Maine being given back to the Indians," he said. "I have no doubt that many people were sincere in wanting the Indians to have their day in court. I also happen to think that just beneath the surface of all the talk about fairness lurked the comforting conviction that, as always, the Indians were bound to lose. In any event, complacency proved to be a tremendous asset for us during 1973 and 1974, because it allowed Passamaquoddy v. Morton to be litigated in a calm, almost academic manner, in an atmosphere that was entirely lacking in emotion or hysteria. During this period, for example, nobody seemed to pay much attention when the Supreme Court not only reversed two lower courts' dismissals of the land claim brought by the Oneida Indian Nation but swept away the argument presented by the County of Oneida that the Nonintercourse Act did not apply in the states that had evolved from the original thirteen colonies. Surprisingly, this atmosphere continued to prevail even when Judge Gignoux finally ruled in our favor. By that time, some of us were beginning to wonder just how long it would take for the citizens of Maine to consider the Indians' land claim seriously."

Judge Gignoux rendered his opinion in Passamaquoddy v. Morton on January 20, 1975, declaring that the Nonintercourse Act was applicable to the Passamaquoddy Tribe in spite of its lack of federal recognition, that the act established a trust relationship between the United States and the tribe, and that the defendants could not deny the plaintiffs' request for litigation on their behalf on the ground that no such relationship existed. These findings were appealed by the defendants, and while the appeal was being argued and decided—a process that took up most of the rest of the year—the Indian land claim was again shielded from public view. Strangely, it did not surface even when the United States Court of Appeals for the First Circuit, on December 23rd, unanimously upheld Judge Gignoux's decision; indeed, this event went largely unreported by the press. Tureen and his colleagues, for their part, were delighted at the lack of fanfare. They now waited anxiously to see if the federal government or the State of Maine would petition the Supreme Court to review the appellate court's decision by March 22, 1976—the deadline for such a request. The deadline passed without a petition's being filed, and Judge Gignoux's decision in Passamaquoddy v. Morton automatically became law.

At that point, the government was confronted with the problem of deciding the extent of its trust obligation to the Indians in Maine. Within a few weeks, the Commissioner of the Bureau of Indian Affairs announced that the Passamaquoddies and the Penobscots were eligible to receive five million dollars a year in federal benefits for housing, education, health care, and other social services. At the same time, lawyers in the Solicitor's Office of the Department of the Interior quietly began to study the question of whether the government should go ahead with the protective action, and, if so, whether it should expand the scope of the suits that had been filed in the Indian's behalf, and proceed to sue the State of Maine and many of its citizen title-holders for the actual return of some twelve and a half million acres of the Indians' aboriginal territory.

Knowing that such a move was under consideration, Tureen decided that the time might be ripe to negotiate a settlement. "A negotiated settlement had always been a major part of our game plan," he told me. "It was inconceivable to me that rational people could allow a case of this magnitude to be ultimately resolved in court. Since the preliminary legal skirmishes had indicated that there was merit in the theories that underlay our case, it was certainly possible that the tribes might prevail upon the merits—an outcome that no responsible defendant, especially a public one, could possibly risk. By the same token, given the novelty of the claims and the inherent risk of prejudice created by their age and size, it seemed equally obvious that responsible tribal leaders would not turn down a settlement that would insure them a substantial land base. Of course, these rational assumptions of mine had to be balanced against the knowledge that while Indians had won plenty of moral victories in the courts, no tribe had ever obtained the return of any significant amount of land."

During the spring of 1976, Tureen got in touch with a number of prominent officials and attempted to discuss the case with them. The results were disappointing. Governor James Longley—an independent populist and antitax crusader, who had assumed office in January of 1975—refused to consider the Indian land claim a serious matter. State Attorney General Joseph Brennan—a liberal Democrat who had his eye on the governorship—was unwilling to commit himself until he saw which way the popular Longley was going. Officials of the Great Northern Nekoosa Corporation—owner of more than two million acres in the claim area, and by far the largest landholder in the state—informed Tureen that they failed to see how their company was involved in the affair. Eventually, convinced that none of these people were prepared to believe that the federal government would carry out the law and act as a proper trustee for the Indians, Tureen dropped his attempt to open negotiations and spent the summer helping the Interior Department, which was studying the historical and legal basis of his clients' claim to nearly two-thirds of the state of Maine.

By September, word that the Indian land suit included the claim that the tribes had civil jurisdiction over their ancestral territories reached Ropes & Gray—a Boston law firm that acts as legal adviser to issuers of New England municipal bonds—and toward the end of the month Ropes & Gray let it be known that it would no longer be able to give unqualified approval to municipal bonds issued within the disputed area. Within a few days, the sale of more than twenty-seven million dollars in bonds for cities, towns, hospitals, and school districts was either cancelled or delayed, and reports began to circulate that people living there might soon find it impossible to transfer real estate or get mortgages.

On September 29th, in an attempt to forestall the growing financial crisis, Governor Longley flew to Washington and met with the members of the Maine congressional delegation, who, in spite of Tureen's protest that their action was disgraceful, and might even be unconstitutional, introduced resolutions in the House and Senate directing the federal courts to refuse to hear any claim that might be brought for return of the Indians' aboriginal territory. However, Congress adjourned before the resolutions could be voted on, and the rest of the autumn was devoted to a war of nerves, whose rhetoric was reported in newspaper articles that, as often as not, were accompanied by maps showing two-thirds of Maine marked by the kind of cross-hatching used to depict zones of military occupation. To begin with, Governor Longley, who insisted on repeatedly referring to the threat to people's homes even though the tribes had repeatedly stated that they had no intention of taking anyone's home, publicly asked the Indians to limit their claims to monetary damages, and not to seek the return of any land. Tureen responded by pointing out that the Governor's request was legally impossible, since one must establish a right to possess the land before damages can be awarded. Tureen also declared that both hundred-and-fifty-million-dollar damage suits pending merely represented rent owed the Indians by the state for its illegal occupation of the land, and that it would take twenty-five *billion* dollars to indemnify the Passamaquoddies and the Penobscots fully for the loss of their aboriginal territory. Finally, Tureen offered to negotiate an out-of-court settlement that "as a matter of grace would not seek to dispossess any landowner," but this offer was turned down by Attorney General Brennan and Governor Longley. The Attorney General declared that the land claim was without merit, and that the Indians had no worthwhile legal case to bring into court. The Governor described the claim as blackmail, and said that an out-of-court settlement could pose a gross injustice to the citizens of Maine, who were innocent of any wrongdoing.

Such objections notwithstanding, when the Interior Department sent a draft of its long-awaited litigation report to the Justice Department, on January 11, 1977, the Indian land claim suddenly made headlines in newspapers across the nation, for the report recommended that ejectment actions be filed in behalf of the Passamaquoddies and the Penobscots against the three hundred and fifty thousand people who were estimated to be living within the twelve-and-a-half-million-acre region claimed by the Indians and also against all the large paper and timber companies, whose vast holdings had long made them the dominant economic and political force in Maine. In the face of this unexpected development, Governor Longley and Attorney General Brennan quickly issued statements pointing out that the proposals of the Interior Department would be subject to review by the incoming Carter Administration. Then the Governor appealed to the Indians to accept a substitute lawsuit in which they could win only the difference between what they had been paid for their lands nearly two hundred years earlier and what they should have been paid according to the fair-market values of that time. Meanwhile, the Attorney General asked the members of the Maine congressional delegation to introduce a bill that would force such a substitution on the Indians. Brennan's action drew a bitter response from Tureen, who was quoted in the Bangor *Daily News* the following day as saying, "The attorney general would have Congress unilaterally extinguish the Indians' property rights, lock them out of the federal courts, and shunt them into the Indian Claims Commission. Apparently, he feels that the state need only live within the legal system so long as it doesn't prove burdensome, and that when it does the state can either ignore the law or retroactively change it."

When the Interior Department's request for litigation on behalf of the Indians reached the Justice Department, it went to the desk of Peter Taft—a grandson of President Taft and a nephew of Senator Robert Taft—who had been appointed head of the Land and Natural Resources Division at the Justice Department by President Ford. A tough-minded and principled attorney, who was widely respected within the department, Taft immediately came under heavy pressure from

Maine's senior senator, Edmund S. Muskie, to back away from the issue, but he refused to do so. Instead, in a lengthy memo to Judge Gignoux, he set out in detail his reasons for rejecting the state's arguments. He said that the Indians had a valid legal claim to between five and eight million acres of forestland in northern Maine, and announced that unless an out-of-court settlement was reached by June 1st he intended to file test lawsuits against a limited number of major landowners; that meant the giant timber and paper companies, whose holdings in the claim area constituted the largest contiguous privately owned forest in the world. He closed by urging an out-of-court settlement, and by describing the Indian claim as "potentially the most complex litigation ever brought in the federal courts, with social and economic impacts without precedent, and incredible potential litigation costs to all parties."

Toward the end of February, the predicament of the lawyers at Justice was eased somewhat when the Passamaquoddies and the Penobscots agreed not to press their claims for two million acres of heavily populated land along the coast of Maine, on the condition that legislation be passed by the federal government allowing them to sue "an appropriate sovereign" for the monetary value of the land and for trespass damages. And, as a further indication of their willingness to compromise, the Indians agreed not to include in any such substitute remedy their land or damage claims against any homeowner or other small-property owner anywhere else in Maine. On the other hand, they would not relinquish their claim for the return of millions of acres of forestland held by Maine's giant landowners, or the six hundred thousand acres still held by the state itself, which the Justice Department intended to include in its test suit.

On March 1st, the Maine congressional delegation responded to the Justice Department's announcement by introducing identical bills in the House and Senate to extinguish all aboriginal title that might be held by the Passamaquoddy and Penobscot tribes and to limit to monetary damages any claim that the Indians might bring. (In addition to Senator Muskie, the delegation now included Senator Hathaway, who had defeated Senator Smith in 1972; Representative William Cohen, who won the seat vacated by Hathaway that same year; and Representative David Emery, who had defeated Kyros in 1974.) A few days later, Senator James Abourezk, of South Dakota, the chairman of the Senate Select Committee on Indian Affairs, denounced the proposed extinguishment legislation as "a very one-sided attempt to obviate and preclude any just claim on the part of the tribes." After commending the Indians for their efforts to negotiate the issue in a reasonable manner, Abourezk declared that he would not hold hearings on the bill. Shortly thereafter, to the vast relief of practically everyone involved, President Carter announced that he was appointing William B. Gunter, a fifty-seven-year-old Georgia Supreme Court justice who was about to resign, as his special representative to evaluate the claims.

From Tureen's point of view, the entry of the White House into the land-claim case could not have been more timely or fortunate. "In the winter of 1977, we found ourselves sailing into some very deep and uncharted waters," he said recently as he recalled the events that preceded President Carter's decision to intervene. "Ever since the bond crisis of the previous autumn, Governor Longley had taken an increasingly hard-line and demogogic approach to the problem—accusing the Indians of blackmailing the innocent people of Maine, and so forth—and he had become phenomenally popular in the state as a result. In fact, by the end of 1976 the Governor was well on his way to building himself a constituency made up of virtually all the white property owners and paper-mill workers in Maine. The lesson in all this was hardly lost on Attorney General Brennan, who wanted to succeed Governor Longley in the State House in Augusta—or, for that matter, on the members of the Maine congressional delegation, whom Brennan was putting pressure on to pursue legislation that would wipe out the Indians' claim for return of land."

In December, fearing that an attempt to extinguish the claim was imminent, Tureen decided to look for help to counteract it. "We needed a strong ally with impeccable legal credentials and incontestable integrity," he said. "With that in mind, I picked up the telephone one morning and called Professor Archibald Cox, of the Harvard Law School, who, because of his role as the first special prosecutor in the Watergate case, had come to be widely regarded as symbolizing the best in our legal system. After telling him a bit about the land-claim case in Maine, I asked if I might come and talk with him. He said yes, so the next day Barry Margolin and I climbed into my airplane —I had bought it in 1974, in order to get around to my far-flung clients—and flew to Boston. When we arrived in Cambridge, I told Professor Cox that something disgraceful for our nation was being cooked up in the form of legislation to extinguish the Indians' right to reclaim their land, and that I needed his help to defeat it. He told me he would think the matter over. A few weeks later, he agreed to volunteer his services as co-counsel, saying that the Indian land claim was something that involved the national honor.

"When it was announced that Professor Cox had joined us, Governor Longley held a press conference and accused me of orchestrating a public-relations campaign through the news media in an attempt to force an out-of-court settlement of the case. Not long afterward, the Governor announced that he had retained Edward Bennett Williams, the Washington trial lawyer, to represent him in the matter and to act as his personal representative in dealings with the White House and the Department of Justice. That was fine with me, because it meant that Governor Longley would at long last be getting some first-rate legal advice. As for President Carter, he had decided by then to get his legal advice on the land case from Judge Gunter, a man he knew and trusted. Can you imagine the President's dilemma at that point? There he was, brand-new to office, deeply mistrustful of the Washington establishment, and suddenly facing one of the largest, most complex, and politically sensitive lawsuits ever to hit the federal judiciary. What he desperately needed to know from Judge Gunter was whether the Maine Indian claims constituted bona fide lawsuits that the tribes might win in court, and that the federal government should help settle out of court, or whether they were frivolous claims that would certainly be dismissed by the court. My colleagues and I were delighted to have Judge Gunter on the scene. We had felt from the very beginning that if the land-claim case went our way in court it would eventually have to be settled with public funds, and now that push was finally coming to shove we were hopeful that once the government found itself in a position of having to choose between bringing suit against three hundred and fifty thousand citizens of Maine—a form of legal cannibalism—and contributing to an out-of-court settlement, it would opt for the latter course."

During the next three months, representatives of both sides met with Judge Gunter on several occasions in the White House and provided him with a great deal of legal and historical material to support their differing positions. "The basic argument set forth by Professor Cox, Stuart Ross, and me was that, thanks to the court's decision in Passamaquoddy v. Morton, the Indians had a good legal claim to between five and ten million acres of land in Maine," Tureen said.

"We told Judge Gunter that the tribes were willing to negotiate a fair out-of-court settlement, but only on the condition that it included a significant land base for them. We also warned him that any attempt to extinguish the Indian claim without the agreement of the tribes would bring disgrace upon the Carter Administration and the nation. Attorney General Brennan, on the other hand, told Judge Gunter that the federal government had not defended itself adequately in Passamaquoddy v. Morton, and cited new evidence assembled by Professor Ronald Banks, a historian at the University of Maine, to support the contention that the Nonintercourse Act did not apply to the Passamaquoddy and Penobscot tribes but only to Indians living west of the frontier that existed in 1790. When all was said and done, however, Judge Gunter had not been brought in to decide the legal merits of the case. He had been brought in to figure out what our chances of winning might be, and to put a price tag on a settlement. He soon found out that that was not going to be easy. At our second meeting, early in April, he raised the question of money as if it were going to pose a major problem. Professor Cox and I told him that if that was the case we were perfectly willing to take eight million acres and skip the cash. Judge Gunter nearly fell out of his chair. I think it may have been the first time he realized that we meant business. Up to that point, he had been extremely cordial, but from then on he was rather testy. I could hardly blame him. On the one hand, he had to face the fact that our clients had a claim worth billions of dollars and at least a fifty-fifty chance of winning the case in court. On the other hand, he knew very well that the President's Office of Management and Budget was not going to let him give away the federal treasury in order to settle the case out of court. In the end, he had no choice except to pick some numbers out of his hat and come down somewhere in the middle."

On July 15th, Judge Gunter sent President Carter a four-page report that contained an analysis of the land-claim dispute and a solution to it. To begin with, Judge Gunter concluded that the Indian lawsuits, because of their potentially devastating economic impact on the state of Maine, should not be allowed to proceed to trial. Then, after pointing out that the federal government was primarily responsible for creating the problem, he advised the President to recommend that Congress take certain steps: appropriate twenty-five million dollars for the use and benefit of the Passamaquoddy and Penobscot tribes; require the State of Maine to put together and convey to the federal government, as trustee for the two tribes, a hundred-thousand-acre tract of land within the claim area; assure the tribes that normal Bureau of Indians Affairs benefits would be provided to them in the future; request the state to continue providing benefits to the Indians worth just over a million dollars a year; and require the Secretary of the Interior to use his best efforts to acquire long-term options on four hundred thousand more acres in the claim area, which could then be bought by the tribes at fair market value with their own funds. Judge Gunter recommended that if the two tribes refused to accept these proposals Congress immediately extinguish their aboriginal title to all privately owned lands within the claim area, more than ninety-five percent of the total claim, and allow the Indians to sue for only some five hundred thousand acres held in public ownership by the State of Maine. Gunter went on to recommend that if, conversely, the state refused to accept his proposals, Congress pay twenty-five million dollars to the Indians and then proceed to extinguish their claim to all privately owned lands, with the idea that they would still be able to sue Maine for the public lands that remained.

As might be expected, Judge Gunter's proposals for settling the land-claim case received mixed notices. At first look, President Carter found them to be "fair, very judicious, and wise." The members of the Maine congressional delegation were somewhat less enthusiastic; they issued a statement describing the plan as "an initial step toward resolution of a very complex issue." Elsewhere on Capitol Hill, reactions ranged from that of Senator Abourezk, who accused Judge Gunter of "recommending that the legal rights of the Indian Tribes be arbitrarily taken away by Congress," to that of Representative Teno Roncalio, of Wyoming, the chairman of the House Indian Affairs Subcommittee, who urged the tribes not to reject the proposals out of hand and warned them about the possibility of an anti-Indian backlash in Congress. Attorney General Brennan, for his part, was gratified that the federal government would be footing the bill for the twenty-five-million-dollar fund and that privately owned lands would be protected, but he was extremely unhappy about the state's being required to contribute a hundred thousand acres—a fifth of its landholdings within the claim area—to the settlement. Governor Longley, who was also distressed by this requirement, called on President Carter to apply the same human-rights standards he advocated in international affairs to the resolution of the land-claim case in Maine, and declared that any out-of-court settlement should be the sole responsibility of the federal government. President Carter was taken to task for a different reason by five former Commissioners of the Bureau of Indian Affairs, the president of the Maine Bar Association, and a number of civil-rights and human-rights activists. They were among seventy-five people recruited by Suzan Harjo, a lobbyist for NARF in Washington, who was a close friend of, and adviser to, Tureen, and they signed a telegram that urged President Carter to reject Judge Gunter's plan. "IT IS UNFORTUNATE ENOUGH THAT JUDGE GUNTER DID NOT SERVE AS A MEDIATOR," the telegram read, in part. "BUT TO SAY THAT THE INDIANS MUST ACCEPT HIS PROPOSAL OR FACE EXTIN-GUISHMENT OF THEIR CLAIMS BY THE POLITICAL BRANCHES IS TO MAKE A MOCKERY OF THIS NATION'S LEGAL AND MORAL OBLIGATIONS TO INDIANS AND TO TELL THE WORLD THAT THE UNITED STATES IS UNWILLING TO ABIDE BY THE DICTATES OF ITS OWN LEGALLY CON-STITUTED COURTS." Perhaps the most down-to-earth comment came from Francis Nicholas, governor of the Passamaquoddies at Pleasant Point, who was also upset by Judge Gunter's extinguishment rec-ommendation. "We spent five years getting the courts to force the federal government to act as our trustee," Nicholas observed. "Now this man says that if we don't accept his terms, the President should protect the big timber companies by taking away our rights. I just don't understand it."

Tureen's view of Judge Gunter's recommendations was both pos-itive and negative. "On the plus side, I looked at them as providing a point of departure for serious negotiations," he said. "And not a bad starting point at that. After all, a hundred thousand acres was far more than any other Indian tribe had ever won, and twenty-five million dollars was at least eighty times as much as my clients could ever have hoped to be awarded in an Indian Claims Commission proceeding. Moreover, I felt sure that if we could just get to the bargaining table we would be able to improve upon the offer, simply because Judge Gunter's recommendations contained some elements that greatly en-hanced our position. For one thing, he had obviously acknowledged that the Passamaquoddies and the Penobscots had a substantial claim to the land in Maine. And, even more important, he had adopted my clients' basic premise that there could be no settlement without a significant amount of land. This was a crucial concession, because terms such as these had never been agreed to by the government in an Indian case. For these contributions, Judge Gunter should have been highly commended. As for his take-it-or-leave-it threat to wipe out most of the claim if the Indians did not go along with his plan, that was another matter. Judge Gunter was there reverting to the highly prejudiced theory of law that had been brought to North America by the Europeans, who, practically from the moment they arrived on these shores, took the position that they could terminate the Indians' aboriginal title at their pleasure. What Judge Gunter was proposing was that if the two tribes refused to accept his deal the government should retroactively validate all the grossly unfair and illegal transactions by which Massachusetts and Maine had ripped off millions of acres of the tribes' land in direct violation of the Nonintercourse Act. Judge Gunter was playing the role of the godfather. His proposal was presented as an offer we could not refuse. It seemed to us that the very fact that he could recommend something so unconstitutional was a pretty good indication of the extent to which the Maine Indian land-claim case was pushing the limits of the judicial system, and of how close the keepers of that system were to abandoning their principles. The Passamaquoddies and the Penobscots were now being warned, in effect, that if they pushed the federal government any further, it would resort to the tactics of the frontier days. In that event, the Indians would have found themselves reliving the invasion of North America by the white man. Thanks to President Carter, this did not happen. The President, who obviously felt compelled to treat the Indians honorably, backed away from this aspect of Judge Gunter's recommendations, and the White House announced the creation of a three-man task force to sit down and talk with them."

President Carter's task force, which was known as the White House Work Group, was appointed in October of 1977, even as rumors were circulating in Washington that Edward Bennett Williams, who would soon withdraw from the case, had advised Governor Longley and Attorney General Brennan to settle the land-claim dispute rather than risk a catastrophic loss in court. The Work Group was made up of Eliot R. Cutler, a native of Bangor and a former legislative assistant to Senator Muskie and then the associate director for Natural Resources, Energy, and Science at the Office of Management and Budget; Leo M. Krulitz, the Solicitor of the Department of the Interior; and A. Stephens Clay, a Washington attorney who was a partner in Judge Gunter's law firm. Over the next several months, the group held eight meetings with an eleven-man Pasamaquoddy-Penobscot Negotiating

Committee, which included the tribal governors of the Passama-quoddy reservations at Indian Township and Pleasant Point, the tribal governor of the Penobscots, and eight other members of the two tribes, who had been elected to serve on it by their tribes. The meetings, which were boycotted by the State of Maine, took place in the West Wing of the White House and in the Old Executive Office Building, and although they initially dealt with technical questions involving the kind of assistance that would be extended to the tribes by the Bureau of Indian Affairs, they were almost immediately expanded to include the Indians' land and damage claims.

"Late in October, when we got down to realistic bargaining, we told the Work Group that the hundred thousand acres proposed by Judge Gunter would not provide a sufficient land base for the two tribes, and was simply unacceptable," Tureen said. "We asked, in-stead, for five hundred thousand acres. The Work Group came back with an offer of two hundred and twenty-five thousand acres, and in the end we compromised at three hundred thousand. The big question was, of course, where was all this real estate going to come from? At that point, the White House people proposed that the additional land be acquired from the holdings of the large paper companies, which until then had been allowed to remain pretty well out of the whole dispute. Since it had been obvious for some time that the paper and timber companies, which owned vast unoccupied areas in Maine, would undoubtedly be major defendants in any lawsuit, we were only too happy to go along with this idea. The result was a joint memo-randum of understanding between the Passamaquoddy-Penobscot Ne-gotiating Committee and the White House Work Group, which was signed in early February of 1978."

Under the terms of the joint memorandum of understanding, the Carter Administration agreed to ask Congress for legislation to provide the Passamaquoddy and Penobscot tribes with twenty-five million dollars for their trust fund. In return, the two tribes agreed to the extinguishment of their claim against all title holders with fifty thousand acres or less in the claim area. This agreement would have automatically cleared title to more than nine million acres in the twelve-and-a-half-million-acre region that had been deemed to be the Indians' aboriginal territory. What remained in dispute was three hundred and fifty thousand acres held by the State of Maine and approximately three million acres held by fourteen large private landholders, in-cluding the Great Northern Nekoosa Corporation, the International

Paper Company, the Boise Cascade Corporation, the Georgia-Pacific Corporation, the Diamond International Corporation, the Scott Paper Company, and the St. Regis Paper Company. Under the terms of the memorandum, the two tribes agreed to dismiss their claims against Maine in exchange for the assurance that the state would continue to appropriate a million seven hundred thousand dollars a year for them over the next fifteen years. As for the fourteen large private land-holders, the Indians agreed to dismiss all trespass claims against them in return for three hundred thousand acres of average-quality timberland and long-term options to buy two-hundred thousand acres more at fair market value. To facilitate this part of the bargain, the Carter Administration agreed to recommend that Congress pay a million and a half dollars to the landholders contributing acreage and options to the settlement package—a sum that came to about five dollars an acre—and to contribute three and a half million dollars more for the two tribes in order to help them exercise the long-term options.

Reaction in Maine to the joint memorandum of understanding, which soon became known throughout the state as the White House Plan, ranged from expressions of outrage to calls for violence. One lawmaker in Augusta vented his wrath on the members of President Carter's Work Group by declaring that "someone should get a gun and shoot those bastards." A state senator from the claim area announced that he was going to "invest heavily in Winchesters and Remingtons." Attorney General Brennan said that the recommendations of the memorandum were "irresponsible and indefensible." Governor Longley accused the Carter Administration of treating the state's officials "very shabbily." He described the proposed settlement as the "second dealing of a stacked deck," and likened the plan to something that could be expected to emanate from Red China. Samuel Casey, the chairman of the Great Northern Nekoosa Corporation, rejected the plan on the ground that it discriminated unfairly against his company, and members of the United Paperworkers International Union sent postcards to members of the Maine congressional delegation opposing the settlement because it might have an adverse economic impact on the paper industry. As for the delegation, it was sharply divided on the proposal. Representatives Cohen and Emery attacked the plan as an attempt to pit small landowners against the large paper companies, while Senators Muskie and Hathaway urged state officials to give it serious consideration. A further indication of the explosiveness of the issue occurred when Senator Hathaway, who said that the plan provided a fair approach, offered to act as broker in an out-of-court settlement and proposed that the government's per-acre payments to the paper companies and other larger landowners be substantially increased: he was immediately the target of a public attack by Governor Longley, who accused him of advocating a giveaway of private land and tax dollars.

Aware that little progress could be made in settling the land-claim case in such an environment, Tureen and his Indian clients spent the rest of the winter waiting for the protest to subside and the political infighting to die down. "It was a very nasty and disillusioning period in Maine," Tureen said. "Indian children were harassed at school, there was a big run on guns at the sporting-goods stores, and after a number of threats were made against my life I even carried a gun myself for a while. The chief reason for all the bitterness was that the agreement we signed with the White House people had greatly strengthened our hand. For one thing, it contained the unwritten but evident understanding that unless the large paper companies agreed to an out-of-court settlement the Justice Department would proceed to file suit against them. For another, it contained a tacit agreement on the part of President Carter to support a negotiated settlement of the problem, as opposed to Longley's plan to extinguish the claim. This effectively killed the chances for such a wipeout, because it would have to be accomplished over a Presidential veto—something that, as a practical matter, was politically impossible. The President made his position on this score very clear at a town meeting he held in Bangor, on February 17th, when he stated that he would veto any legislation that was not the product of negotiations and that attempted to abolish the Indian land-claim suit. At that point, no public figure in Maine should have doubted that the President had decided not to follow Judge Gunter's recommendation for extinguishment. The trouble was that many of the state's politicians had by then determined that the best way to make political hay in the coming November elections was by taking a hard-line, anti-Indian stand on the land-claim issue."

During the early spring of 1978, a great deal of maneuvering occurred as both sides in the dispute sought to influence public opinion. Representative Cohen, who had decided to run for the Senate against Hathaway, charged that the White House had allowed Tureen to formulate the terms of the proposed settlement, and called for a

Supreme Court ruling on the applicability of the Nonintercourse Act to the Indians in Maine. Tureen responded by reminding Cohen that if the Court ruled in favor of the tribes there would be little incentive for them to settle for only three hundred thousand acres, since they would then be free to press for return of the entire twelve and a half million acres of their aboriginal territory. Attorney General Brennan, who had announced his candidacy to succeed Governor Longley in January, reiterated his belief that the Indian lawsuit was unsound and that the proposed settlement was unfair to large landhholders. Tureen countered by suggesting that if that was the case the state should offer to defend the paper companies in court and indemnify them if they lost. Tureen went on to point out that if the chances of the Indians' winning were really, as Brennan had claimed, "so remote as to be inconceivable," such a proposal could not conceivably cost the state any money. This was too much for Longley, who issued a statement attacking Tureen for making proposals that would take unfair advantage of Maine's taxpayers.

Late in April, the land-claim case took a new turn when, after a plea from Presidential Counsel Robert Lipshutz, Governor Longley and Attorney General Brennan did an abrupt about-face and declared that they were ready to open negotiations with Tureen and the tribal negotiating committee for an out-of-court settlement. Talks began on April 26th but soon broke down over the question of whether the Passamaquoddy and Penobscot tribes should be exempt from state taxes and from state criminal and civil laws, and Governor Longley stalked out of the final meeting charging that the Indians were conspiring to establish "a nation within a nation." With the negotiations at an impasse, United States Attorney General Griffin Bell decided in June that the Justice Department would sue Maine for three hundred and fifty thousand acres and three hundred million dollars as the first phase of its prosecution of the land-claim case. In August, however, the Attorney General surprised almost everyone by informing Judge Gignoux that the Department would not file suit against the fourteen large landholders, on the ground that it was unfair to make any distinction between large landowners and small landowners in the claim area.

Tureen and his colleagues were taken aback by Bell's unexpected decision, which was widely heralded in Maine as a welcome repudiation of the proposed settlement that had been negotiated and signed by President Carter's White House Work Group, and as a vindication of the hard-line position that had been taken against it by Governor Longley and Attorney General Brennan. In a public statement, Tureen confidently pointed out that Bell's action had little legal significance, because, thanks to several recent court decisions involving other Eastern Indian tribes that he and his colleagues were handling, the Passamaquoddies and the Penobscots were free to go ahead and sue private landholders on their own. Privately, however, he was extremely worried. "We knew that Attorney General Bell was an unpredictable man, who often operated independently of his staff, and who considered the Justice Department to be a fourth branch of the government," Tureen said. "We also knew that, with the departure of Bert Lance, Bell was the closest man in the Cabinet to the President. So, naturally, we wondered if this latest move on his part was a signal that the Carter Administration was getting ready to desert us. In order to find out which way the wind was blowing, I went to Washington late in August and met with Senators Muskie and Hathaway in Muskie's hideaway office at the Capitol. What they had to say was rather distressing. They told me that if President Carter sent legislation to Congress based upon the joint memorandum of understanding, they might well be forced to go along with a congressional amendment that would settle the land-claim case on terms unfavorable to the Indians. This was out-and-out arm-twisting, of course, and I realized as much when, following the meeting in Muskie's office, Senator Hathaway told me that a negotiated settlement might still be possible if the Indians would agree to accept a hundred thousand acres and twenty-five million dollars. Hathaway said he thought he might be able to persuade Congress and the President to appropriate twenty-five million dollars for the trust fund that the two tribes had already agreed to accept in return for extinguishment of their claim against small landholders, and ten million dollars more for land acquisition. This, he felt, plus two million dollars, which he thought might be furnished by the State of Maine, would enable the tribes to buy a hundred thousand acres from the big paper companies at fair market value. I told Senator Hathaway that my clients would never agree to such a settlement. I pointed out that they had negiotiated in good faith with the White House Work Group, that three hundred thousand acres was their bottom line, and that they expected the President's representatives to keep their word in the bargain they had made. The whole business left me wondering if Muskie or Hathaway or both had not put Bell up to his statements in an effort to get my clients to settle more cheaply. In fact, I even considered sharing my suspicion with Hathaway, for whom I had high regard and whom I liked personally. Instead, I reminded him that he was the only member of the Maine congressional delegation who had declared that the joint memorandum of understanding provided a fair approach to the land-claim problem, and I pointed out that Bell's apparent repudiation of it had seriously undermined his position, and could even hurt his chances for reëlection."

In the second week of September, Attorney General Bell made another surprise move: he asked Judge Gignoux to grant the Justice Department a six-month delay in pressing the Indian land-claim case against the State of Maine. In his petition to the court, Bell called for Congress to intercede and settle the issue, and took the highly unusual step of promising that he would become personally involved in the drafting of new legislation to resolve the dispute. At the time, press reports attributed Bell's abrupt turnabout to a belated awareness on the part of the Carter Administration that a government lawsuit against Maine less than two months before the November election would surely jeopardize Senator Hathaway's chances for reëlection. There was also speculation that Bell's action indicated that the Administration might be ready to move toward a totally federally financed resolution of the case. Both surmises proved to be correct, as Tureen discovered toward the end of the month, when Senator Hathaway telephoned him from Washington.

"By that time, Hathaway was in deep political trouble because of the Indian issue," Tureen said. "Representative Cohen, his opponent, who was running television ads suggesting that Hathaway was willing to give a large part of Maine back to the Indians, held a big lead in the polls, and Hathaway realized that if he did not come up with a solution to the land-claim dispute before November he was going to lose the election. During our conversation, he told me that he had discussed the problem with President Carter's Counsel, Robert Lipshutz, and that while Lipshutz had agreed in principle to a federal resolution of the case, he had refused to commit the Adminstration to any settlement costing more than thirty-five million dollars, on the ground that the budget ceiling would not permit a higher appropiation. At that point, I realized it would be foolish of me to turn Senator Hathaway down a second time, for, given the political realities in Maine, a federally financed settlement was the only way to resolve the land-claim case short of going to court—which neither side wanted to do, for the simple reason that both had too much to lose. The question was how to modify the existing proposal so that it would be acceptable to both sides. Since it was obviously necessary for Senator Hathaway to come up with a plan in which the Carter Administration would not appear to be footing the whole bill with federally appropriated funds, I suggested that he explore ways in which extra money for my clients to buy land might be made available from existing government programs. I pointed out to the Senator that this not only would allow the White House to save face on the budget issue but also would allow him to frame his settlement package in such a way that the voters of Maine, who had been whipped into an anti-Indian frenzy during the election campaign, would not see it as a politically motivated federal giveaway. The Senator was enthusiastic about the idea. But I then had to tell him that there was no way the full membership of the Passamaquoddy and Penobscot tribes could ratify a settlement before Election Day, and that the very best I could do was place any new proposal he might make before the members of the negotiating committee, and ask them to say publicly that it was a constructive offer. The Senator said this was acceptable to him, and over the next week we discussed the terms under which it might be accomplished."

Tureen went on to say that what they ended up with could best be described as an agreement consisting of a public understanding and a private understanding. The public understanding, which Senator Hathaway put before the voters of Maine, called for the Indians to agree to the extinguishment of all their claims in return for a twenty-seven-million-dollar federal appropriation for their trust fund and ten million dollars in additional federal money, with which to buy a hundred thousand acres from the paper companies. The private understanding, which was spelled out in confidential letters sent to Tureen by Leo Krulitz, of the Department of the Interior, called for the Bureau of Indian Affairs to provide the tribes with ten million dollars additional for capital improvements, such as repairs to schools, roads, and bridges, and to make available fifteen million dollars in subsidized loan funds for setting up tribal business ventures and for improving the Indian economy. "Most important of all, we also got Krulitz to agree in writing to help us look for other money in existing federal programs, in order to buy the additional two hundred thousand acres that were needed to make up the three-hundred-thousand-acre land base that the White House people had agreed to in the memorandum of understanding,"

Tureen said. "With Senator Hathaway's assistance, we then made a private agreement with the large paper companies, with whom we had been quietly negotiating for several months, which committed them to selling us a minimum of two hundred thousand acres at fair market value. This still left us a hundred thousand acres short, but we decided we could take our chances on finding that much land on the open market."

In the middle of October, Senator Hathaway announced his plan for ending the ten-year-old land-claim dispute, but he made no mention of the private understanding that had been reached between the Indians and the Interior Department. As a result, newspapers from one end of Maine to the other described the proposed settlement as if the Passamaquoddies and the Penobscots had agreed to take only thirty-seven million dollars for the extinguishment of their claim and to accept a hundred thousand acres instead of the three hundred thousand they had been promised under the joint memorandum of understanding. Not surprisingly, each of the politicians involved tried to turn the proposal to his advantage. Senator Hathaway, whose statesmanship was praised by Rosalynn Carter, claimed credit for bringing the Indians, the White House, and the paper companies together and resolving the thorny issue, while Governor Longley, Attorney General Brennan, and Representative Cohen—all of whom supported the new plan—claimed vindication of their stand that Maine should not be held financially accountable in any settlement, and pointed to the fact that the President had finally endorsed a solution that required not a penny of money or a square inch of land from the state. When the election was held, on November 7th, Senator Hathaway lost to Representative Cohen in a landslide, and Attorney General Brennan was an easy winner in the gubernatorial race. Ironically, most political observers felt that the two men had been propelled into office by an anti-Indian backlash vote whose momentum had been augmented at the last moment by the widely held public belief that the state had come out way ahead in the settlement.

After the election, people in Maine generally assumed that the land-claim case was over and done with, and the Indian question dropped out of the headlines. During the winter and early spring of 1979, the paper companies set aside tracts for the two hundred thousand acres they had agreed to make available as their part of the

Hathaway deal, and opened negotiations with Tureen and the nego- tiating committee to sell the land to the Indians at fair market value. Meanwhile, the members of the Passamaquoddy and Penobscot tribes overwhelmingly ratified the Hathaway proposal, which was presented to them as a plan that would provide them with a twenty-seven-million- dollar trust fund and three hundred thousand acres. In April, however, when word that the tribes expected to acquire this much land got back to the Interior Department, Leo Krulitz said that Tureen and the negotiating committee had misunderstood a key part of the Hathaway proposal. According to Krulitz, the government's agreement to look for extra money in federal programs was not intended as a prerequisite for settling the claim case but only as a good-faith offer to help the Indians finance future land purchases.

Aware that they were not in a position to get much mileage out of their private understanding with former Senator Hathaway, Tureen and the members of the negotiating committee reminded Krulitz that the only agreement the committee had made in writing was with the White House Work Group, of which Krulitz had been a member, and that the Work Group had promised the tribes a land base of three hundred thousand acres. "We told him that we needed an additional thirty million dollars to pay for this land base, and that if the money was not forthcoming we were ready to take our case to court," Tureen said. "During the next few weeks, Krulitz and I held a series of meet- ings, but we couldn't come to any agreement. Krulitz had been our friend since he had come to Interior, in early 1977, and he had stood firm on the legal issues throughout our most difficult days with Griffin Bell. But he had always been extremely tight-fisted when it came to money, and when he finally realized that the tribes were serious about holding out for a settlement that would cost over sixty million dollars we lost his support. Krulitz' defection could have had serious conse- quences, of course, but just as the whole settlement plan was about to collapse he withdrew from the negotiations, and a man named Eric Jankel, who had just become Secretary of the Interior Cecil Andrus's assistant for intergovernmental affairs, was brought into the picture. As luck would have it, Jankel and I knew each other. We had met back in 1977, when he was working for Governor Joseph Garrahy of Rhode Island. At that time, we had negotiated an amicable settlement of a land-claim case under which the Narragansett Tribe had received eighteen hundred acres of land. We now sat down with Donald Per- kins, the lawyer who was representing most of the major paper and timber companies, and in very short order the three of us figured out a way to raise the thirty million dollars in the form of grants from the Economic Development Administration and the Small Business Administration and other federal agencies."

At the beginning of August, Perkins, Tureen, and the negotiating committee presented the salvaged settlement package to the members of the Maine congressional delegation, whose approval would be needed if legislation resolving the land-claim case was to be passed by Congress. However, the delegation refused to go along with the latest proposal until it was approved by the State of Maine, which, in turn, refused to sanction it until the question of who would have legal jurisdiction over the two tribes was worked out. In October, therefore, Tureen and the Passamaquoddy-Penobscot Negotiating Committee opened talks with state officials to settle the matter, and these discussions were still in progress in January of 1980, when I visited Tureen at his office in Portland.

"In one sense, this whole issue of jurisdiction has been a red herring," he told me at the time. "At the heart of the problem is the fact that Governor Brennan was elected last autumn on a solemn pledge that the Indians would not get an inch of land or a single penny from the State of Maine. Although the federal government has long offered to foot the whole bill for the land claim, the Governor understands very well that a large settlement will still be highly unpopular in Maine, where he and former Governor Longley have been whipping up anti-Indian sentiment for years. So at this point Brennan is hung up on a dilemma of his own making. In short, he can't very well become the willing partner of a resolution that he has done his best to prevent—a simple matter of saving face. Therefore, jurisdiction has become the pretext by which he hopes to hold up a final settlement of the land claim if it is at all possible to do so. Now, to be fair, it should be understood that the question of jurisdiction is immensely complicated and sensitive. It's a much more thorny issue than either land or money, for example, because it tends to be a matter of principle. To begin with, one must remember that federally recognized Indian tribes occupy a unique legal position, in that the courts recognize them as continuing to retain their original sovereignty over internal tribal affairs except to the extent that their sovereignty has been limited by federal government. Federally recognized tribes have the power to establish their own courts, and, with the exception of the most serious crimes—such as murder, rape, and arson—to adjudicate disputes and criminal matters that arise between tribal members on their reservations. Similarly, Indians are generally considered to be exempt from state regulatory laws, as well as from many state taxes. Indians who live and earn their income on federal reservations, for example, are not obliged to pay state income taxes. Federally recognized Indians are generally immune from state fishing, hunting, and trapping laws. And another important aspect of Indian tribal sovereignty is that non-Indians living on Indian reservations have no constitutional right to any voice in tribal decision-making."

Tureen went on to say that while Indians in the United States had struggled to maintain their inherent sovereignty for hundreds of years the issue had become paramount following the Second World War. "During the nineteen-fifties, the federal government unilaterally terminated the sovereignty of several tribes, including the Menominee of Wisconsin and the Siletz of Oregon, with devastating social, psychological, and economic consequences for their members, which galvanized Indian resistance to further action of this type," he explained. "During the nineteen-sixties, the civil-rights movement generally increased vigilance and militancy on the part of minority groups throughout the nation, and the Office of Economic Opportunity's Legal Services made lawyers available without charge to individual Indians and to small tribes in order to work on the many legal problems and issues that confronted them. Until then, most Indians had seen lawyers only when there was a large claims case to be handled on a contingency-fee basis. The result was a number of lawsuits in which Indian tribes throughout the United States sought to assert or extend jurisdictional rights that had either gone unrecognized or had lain dormant for many years. In some instances, the Indians were stunningly successful—as in the case of the fishing-rights controversy in Washington State, where a group of small tribes won the right to half of the harvestable salmon in all the important rivers in the western part of the state. In another case, however, in which the Supreme Court held that tribal courts had no jurisdiction over non-Indians in criminal cases, the Indians lost. The point is that all this legal activity served to make jurisdiction a central issue for Indians across the nation, so that by the time negotiations began in the Maine Indian land-claim case, in the spring of 1978, the leaders of the Passamaquoddies and the Penobscots were determined to obtain full federal status for their tribes. The trouble was that this placed them on a collision course with the State of Maine, which for a hundred and sixty years had felt that the Passamaquoddy

Tribe and the Penobscot Nation had no inherent sovereign powers, and that Indians could exercise only those powers which the state saw fit to grant them. For his part, Governor Longley had been implacably opposed to granting federal jurisdiction status to the Maine Indians. He was especially outraged by the suggestion that the Indians should not have to pay state taxes. Being an astute politician, he was doubtless aware that several political figures in the state of Washington—among them Attorney General Slade Gorton and Representative Lloyd Meeds—had generated considerable popularity and following by opposing Indian efforts to assert jurisdictional rights through the courts. In any event, during 1977 and 1978 Governor Longley became more and more adamant that there could be no resolution of the Indian claim unless the tribes were totally subject to state jurisdiction, and received no federal status for anything other than the provision of federal services for such things as land management, education, and welfare. Given the respective hard-line positions of the tribes and the state, its's not hard to see how the Maine congressional delegation's decision, in August of 1979, not to place legislation to settle the land-claim case before Congress until it was approved by the State of Maine—which, in turn, refused to give this approval until the jurisdictional issues were resolved—could easily have ended all prospects for a negotiated settlement. In fact, it probably would have, were it not for three incredibly —albeit accidentally—well-timed court decisions that were handed down between May and July of that year. These three decisions—two of them favorable to our clients and one that threatened to reverse our long string of legal victories, and even put an end to the land claim—were directly responsible for the start of serious negotiations between the tribes and the state on the question of jurisdiction at the beginning of October."

Tureen said that the first of the decisions involved John Bottomly, the Boston lawyer whom Don Gellers had brought into the initial land-claim case back in 1968. "Over the years, I have performed almost all of my work for the Maine Indians as the salaried employee of NARF, and Archibald Cox and Stuart Ross have donated their services without charge," Tureen told me. "Don Gellers, however, had a ten-percent contingency-fee contract with the Passamaquoddy Tribe for his lawsuit against Massachusetts, and he subsequently assigned forty percent of his contingency to Bottomly, who, in May of 1978, when our case was making headlines across the nation, filed suit in federal court in Portland, claiming that because of his agreement with Gellers he was entitled to receive four percent of the total value of any settlement the tribe might make. Bottomly's suit had little merit, for a number of reasons. Neither he nor Gellers had ever worked on the claim that was in the process of being settled, and the lawsuit they filed against Massachusetts ten years earlier had gone nowhere. However, Judge Gignoux was not required to deal with the merits of Bottomly's claim. On October 10, 1978, he granted our motion to dismiss Bottomly's action on the grounds that the Maine tribes possessed the same kind of sovereign immunity to civil suit that is enjoyed by federally recognized Indian tribes out west. At that point, the whole business would undoubtedly have died a quiet death if the State of Maine had been willing to leave well enough alone. As things turned out, however, Attorney General Brennan decided that Bottomly's appeal of Judge Gignoux's opinion would provide an ideal opportunity to test a new set of arguments that had been assembled by the Maine Attorney General's Office to prove that Gignoux's 1975 decision in Passamaquoddy v. Morton was wrong."

At this point, Tureen told me that the arguments Brennan wanted to test had been developed by John Paterson, a deputy attorney general, who had taken over responsibility for the land-claim case after the decision in Passamaquoddy, and by Professor Banks, at the University of Maine, whom Paterson had hired. "Paterson and Banks theorized that Maine and the federal government had made a mistake when they defended Passamaquoddy on the ground that the Nonintercourse Act applied only to federally recognized tribes," he said. "So in the winter of 1979, when Bottomly's appeal came up before the United States Court of Appeals for the First Circuit, Maine filed a brief amicus curiae on behalf of Bottomly, and Paterson and Banks raised a whole new interpretation of the act. What they did was produce historical research purporting to show that all of the early federal statutes relating to Indians were intended by Congress to be geographically limited to areas defined as 'Indian country,' which lay to the west of various boundary lines demarking the frontier, and thus excluded New England. In doing so, they tried to get around the Supreme Court's 1974 ruling in the Oneida case—that the Nonintercourse Act applied in the states evolving from the original thirteen colonies—by pointing out that the Court had not specifically considered whether the act applied in those parts of the original thirteen colonies which lay to the east of the Indian boundaries. As a result, they argued that the Passamaquoddy Tribe should not have been

allowed to invoke the federal common-law doctrine of the tribal immunity in its defense against Bottomly's action, because all federal
Indian laws, both statutory and common, applied only to areas outside
New England. We countered by demonstrating that while most federal
Indian statutes—especially those dealing with day-to-day trade—were
limited by their terms to 'Indian country,' the Nonintercourse Act,
which specifically regulated land transactions, was never geographically limited, and applied by its terms to Indian tribes living throughout the United States. What was at issue here was the extent to which
the court was willing to rely on the literal wording of the Nonintercourse Act as passed by Congress in 1790, and to ignore what seemed
to be the common understanding of the meaning of the act on the
part of the people of New England at that time. While courts do not
normally allow common understanding to overcome the plain language
of a statute, the new interpretation of the act which was advanced by
the state made us nervous for the very simple reason that if it were
adopted Passamaquoddy v. Morton would, in effect, be reversed, and
the whole land-claim case would fall into limbo. Happily, we survived
the challenge. In May of 1979, the Court of Appeals issued a unanimous opinion rejecting Maine's new arguments, and reaffirming its
holdings in Passamaquoddy that the terms of the Nonintercourse Act
applied in Maine. And while it was at it the Appeals Court also held
that the Passamaquoddy Tribe possessed the same degree of inherent
sovereignty as any other tribe in the United States."

The Bottomly case was, of course, a major defeat for Maine on
the question of the applicability of the Nonintercourse Act, but as
things turned out the state would be handed an even more humiliating
setback on the same issue the following July 3rd, when the Maine
Supreme Judicial Court rendered its decision in a case called State v.
Dana. Back in May of 1977, Albert C. Dana, a Passamaquoddy Indian
living in Indian Township, and Allen Sockabasin, a charismatic former
governor of the Indian Township Reservation, who would later become
a member of the Passamaquoddy-Penobscot Negotiating Committee,
had been arrested and charged with trying to burn down the reservation's elementary-school building at Peter Dana Point. Later that
year, the two men were tried and convicted of attempted arson by
the State Superior Court in Machias. After the jury had found the
defendants guilty, their attorneys argued that the state court lacked
jurisdiction over the alleged offense, because arson was one of the
class of crimes in which jurisdiction is reserved to the federal govern-

ment under the Indian Major Crimes Act of 1948. The trial judge denied their motion for dismissal, however, and Dana and Sockabasin appealed their conviction to the Maine Supreme Judicial Court, which sat in Bangor on May 7, 1979, with seven of its eight members present, to hear oral argument.

"The courtroom was steaming and packed with Indians from both tribes, as well as with lawyers, reporters, and spectators," Tureen said. "Everyone who was there seemed to understand that history was being made. First of all, great attention had been focused upon the proceedings by the press, and people realized that Dana was a crucially important test of Brennan's contention that the provisions of the Nonintercourse Act did not apply to the Maine Indians, and that the Indian Major Crimes Act was thus also inapplicable within the state. Second, the Maine Supreme Judicial Court had not dealt with an Indian issue since 1892, when it held in State v. Newell—a case involving an Indian who shot two deer out of season in Indian Township—that the Passamaquoddy Tribe had ceased to exist as a sovereign entity. Third, the fact that the Nonintercourse Act and the Major Crimes Act were being addressed in the state's own court for the very first time since the start of the land claim was tremendously important from a political and psychological point of view. And, finally, the very future of the proposed settlement of the land-claim case was once again at stake, for an unfavorable decision from the state's highest court would undoubtedly make meaningful negotiations with the state on the question of jurisdiction, as well as legislation by Congress, impossible until the United States Supreme Court had resolved the issue." Tureen said that as counsel for the Passamaquoddy Tribe he had filed a brief amicus curiae on behalf of the two defendants, and that the United States had filed a similar brief. "Oral argument lasted an exceptionally long time—more than two hours—because of the extraordinary complexity of the case," he told me. "Needless to say, everyone was on pins and needles. John Paterson knew that he needed a knockout punch if Maine was going to stop a settlement of the land claim, which, because of the support of the Carter Administration, was beginning to look more and more like a fait accompli. For our part, we realized that in spite of winning all the previous decisions we could easily lose this one, simply because it is always easy for an appellate court to get rid of a messy case with far-reaching practical and political consequences by affirming a negative decision by a lower court.

"When the proceedings began, Paterson went to the well again with essentially the same argument he had employed in Bottomly a few months earlier, except that in this instance he was arguing that Dana and Sockabasin were not covered by the Indian Major Crimes Act, because that statute applied only where the Nonintercourse Act applied. In so doing, Paterson was deliberately provoking the court to address the central issue of the land-claim case in the context of a criminal appeal. If he had wanted to, he could have defended on far safer ground—for example, by arguing that Peter Dana Point was not 'Indian country' as that term was defined by the Indian Major Crimes Act. However, as I've indicated, Maine had its back to the ropes, and Paterson desperately needed to unload a haymaker. For my part, I also used the same arguments before the Maine Supreme Court that I had used in Bottomly—essentially, that the Nonintercourse Act by its terms applied to Indian tribes throughout the United States—only in this case I also presented the court with an alternative ground that would enable it to decide the case without addressing the difficult Nonintercourse Act issue raised by Paterson. I did this by arguing that the Indian Major Crimes Act applied not only to reservations under the jurisdiction of the United States but to dependent Indian communities as well, and that because the Department of the Interior had decided, in 1976, before the alleged crime of arson was committed, that the Passamaquoddies were eligible for Bureau of Indian Affairs services, they obviously had to be a dependent Indian community. As the morning wore on, it became more and more apparent from the tone of the justices' questions that they were not sympathetic to the argument presented by the state. However, I fully expected that the court would overturn State v. Dana on the easier ground that I had suggested. Instead, to my surprise and delight, on the night of July 3rd, just as I was about to leave on holiday, I learned that, rather than skirting the difficult issues in its opinion, the court had dwelt upon them at length, and had systematically examined and rejected each and every one of the state's contentions. It was a major victory for our side, of course, because it took the wind out of Governor Brennan's sails, and put him on notice that going to trial against us on the land-claim issue would be a dangerous thing to do, and no doubt helped to convince him that an out-of-court settlement might not be such a bad idea after all. Even more important, it served to vindicate the legal position we had taken on the behalf of the Passamaquoddies and the Penobscots, and to show the people of Maine that Indians had been in the right all along."

On July 4th, Tureen flew his wife and their two small children to Whitehead Island, in the Bay of Fundy, where his wife's parents have a summer cottage, and enjoyed a tranquil and triumphant weekend. When he returned to Portland on Monday, however, he learned that the whole land-claim case was once again in jeopardy, because of a new legal wrinkle that threatened to plunge everything into reverse. What had happened was that on June 20th, unbeknownst to the justices of the Maine Supreme Judicial Court, the United States Supreme Court had rendered a decision in a case called Wilson v. Omaha Indian Tribe, which turned out to have tremendous implications concerning the applicability of the Nonintercourse Act. "Wilson involved a comparatively minor land claim by the Omaha Tribe, which had its beginnings when the Missouri River had changed its course, cutting off a portion of the Omaha Tribe's reservation that lay along the Nebraska-Iowa border," Tureen said. "Various parts of this portion of land were subsequently claimed by a landowner named Roy T. Wilson, by R.G.P., Inc., a farming and land-management company, and by the State of Iowa. In 1975, encouraged and assisted by the Bureau of Indian Affairs, the Omahas crossed the river and occupied the territory that had been cut off from the reservation. As the case made its way through the federal courts, the Indians, on the one hand, and Wilson, the R.G.P. corporation, and Iowa, on the other, claimed ownership of the land. In making its claim, however, the Omaha Tribe alleged that it was entitled to the benefit of a special provision of the Indian Trade and Intercourse Act of 1834, which held that where there was an Indian on one side of a property dispute and a white person on the other the burden of proof would always be on the white person, once the Indian had made out a presumption of title from the fact of previous ownership or possession.

"Since the parties in the case included R.G.P., Inc., and the State of Iowa, a question arose as to whether the term 'white person' could be construed to include them. In its June 20th decision, the Supreme Court held that the term 'white person' included the corporation but not the state, saying that disabilities such as the burden-of-proof provision in the 1834 act do not normally run against a state. To buttress this argument, the Court went on to declare that in this case it was particularly unlikely that Congress intended the term 'white person' to include a state, because all the provisions of the 1834 Trade Intercourse Act were limited in their applicability to 'Indian country' as defined in Section 1 of the act, and that 'Indian country' as so defined did not include any land within any state. Incredibly, this argument had not been presented in any briefs, nor had it been raised in oral argument; the Supreme Court had come to it all on its own! And it was, of course, essentially the same argument that Maine had urged on the First Circuit in Bottomly, and on the Maine Supreme Judicial Court in Dana. Thus, if the Supreme Court meant what it said in Wilson, once it got hold of Dana or any other land-claim decision we would be finished. Suffice it to say, when I heard about the decision in Wilson my heart sank."

The next few days were an agony of doubt for Tureen and his colleagues. The offending language that could undo ten years of work was in the Wilson decision, and they had absolutely no way of knowing whether the Supreme Court really meant what it said, and was sending them a warning, or whether the Court's meaning had been misconstrued by some careless or overworked law clerk during the actual writing of the opinion. Especially perplexing to them was the fact that Justice Byron White, who wrote the Wilson opinion, had also written the opinion in Oneida, the highly favorable 1974 decision concerning the Nonintercourse Act, which had been heavily relied upon by all the courts that had previously agreed with the arguments that had been presented on behalf of the Passamaquoddies and the Penobscots. And even more perplexing than that was the fact that Justice White had relied heavily on Oneida in writing Wilson, and that the Wilson opinion, with the exception of the part relating to the land held by the State of Iowa, was favorable to the Indians.

"We now faced the dilemma of whether to let the situation stand or to attempt to get the Supreme Court to modify what it had said," Tureen went on. "On the one hand, there was the language that quite possibly could destroy the chances of the Maine Indians for settling their claim. On the other hand, not only was there very little precedent for requesting modification of the language of a Supreme Court decision that had already been rendered but there was also the danger that if we called the offending language to the Court's attention the Court might very well deny our request for modification with an accompanying opinion indicating that it knew perfectly well what it had said and meant every word of it. Faced with this predicament, I held a series of telephone conferences with Stuart Ross, Robert Pelcyger, of NARF, and Richard Collins, a lawyer for NARF, who had won several recent Supreme Court decisions favoring the Indians. I also called Archibald Cox at his summer home, in Brooksville, Maine.

After anguishing over the problem, we agreed unanimously, albeit reluctantly, that we ought to request a modification of the Court's language in Wilson, and that the request would have a better chance of succeeding if it were sent to the Court by the Solicitor General. Pelcyger then called a friend, Louis Claiborne, a deputy solicitor general who had originally been hired by Cox when he was Solicitor General under President Kennedy, and, in August, Claiborne submitted a motion in the name of the United States, requesting the Court to delete the language of the buttressing reasoning. In his motion, Claiborne explained that the language contradicted that of Oneida, and was incorrect to the extent that it suggested that all of the provisions of the Trade and Intercourse Acts were limited to 'Indian country.' He also took pains to point out to the Court that if the language of the Wilson opinion remained unmodified it could very well undermine efforts to settle the Maine Indian land claim, as well as similar actions in the Eastern part of the United States. In October, however, the Supreme Court denied Claiborne's motion without comment, and from then on we knew we might be up against it.''

By affirming the language of the buttressing reasoning in Wilson v. Omaha Indian Tribe, the Supreme Court applied an imposing counterweight upon the complex mobile of legal decisions and rulings that, up to that point, had been tilting in favor of the Maine Indians. On the one hand, once the decisions in Bottomly and Dana were rendered the state could no longer be confident that its new research would lead to a dismissal of the land claims. On the other hand, after Wilson the tribes had to face the very real prospect that if they did not reach a legislative settlement the Supreme Court might agree to review the Dana decision, and, in the process, not only end their land claims but destroy their jurisdictional victories as well, and place them back where they had been before the 1975 decision in Passamaquoddy v. Morton. It was a prospect that loomed even larger at the beginning of October 1979, when the State of Maine filed its petition for a writ of certiorari in which it asked the Supreme Court to review the Maine Supreme Judicial Court's ruling in Dana.

"It was not any accident that serious negotiations between the two tribes and the state on the question of jurisdiction began shortly thereafter,'' Tureen said. "Indeed, although it was never mentioned during the joint bargaining sessions, the prospect of a Supreme Court showdown hung over the talks like a sword of Damocles. But as the weeks wore on a rather remarkable change began to take place. Little by little, Maine's new attorney general, a Republican named Richard S. Cohen, who is not related to the senator from the state, began to understand and sympathize with the tribes' determination to govern themselves without fear of state intervention. And, little by little, the Indian negotiators began to trust Cohen and attempt to understand what he needed to obtain for the state in a settlement. Basically, each side needed to design a settlement that could be viewed as consistent with its publicly announced philosophy. In order to achieve this, both sides had to make concessions, and, slowly but surely, we began to move major issues from the unresolved to the resolved side of the ledger. For example, the tribes agreed that serious crimes committed by Indians on the reservations would be tried in state courts rather than in federal courts. The tribes also agreed that individual Indians who lived and earned their income on the reservations would pay state income taxes. Moreover, the Indians agreed that Maine's basic regulatory laws, including its environmental laws, would apply on the reservations.

"As for the state, it agreed that the organization and function of the tribal governments, including the decision to grant formal membership in the tribes, would not be subject to state regulation. It also agreed that the Passamaquoddies and the Penobscots should have the same constitutional right as other federally recognized tribes to exclude non-Indians from participation in tribal decision-making. Moreover, the state not only agreed that all Indian lands in Maine would become subject to a special Nonintercourse Act reaffirming that any transaction involving these lands which was not expressly approved by Congress would be invalid but also agreed to severely curtail its power to exercise eminent domain over any Indian lands. Other concessions by Maine included leaving the Indians with the right to regulate their own fishing, hunting, and trapping, with the exception of fishing in navigable rivers, as well as the right to set up tribal courts to deal with misdemeanors and minor infractions committed by Indians against other Indians. For the most part, the discussions with the state were conducted in an atmosphere of mutual respect and compromise, which, considering the bitterness and intransigence that had surrounded the land-claim case in the past, was surprising."

On February 19, 1980, the Supreme Court denied certiorari in the Dana case and thus declined to hear it. By that time, however, the talks between the Indians and the state were going so well that a final settlement seemed within reach. Early in March, a draft of the legislation embodying final agreements concerning jurisdiction was approved by members of the Passamaquoddy-Penobscot Negotiating Committee, and within two weeks it was put to an advisory referendum and ratified by the full membership of both tribes by a majority of about two and one-half to one. The final legislation, which was called the Maine Implementing Act, was introduced in the last week of March, during the closing days of the session of the Maine State Legislature. In spite of an editorial in the Bangor *Daily News* warning that "our lawmakers should not allow themselves to be deluded or intimidated by the arrogance and audacity of the Indians' lawyer, Tom Tureen," and posing the question that "if the Indians get their money and land in Maine, will the Native American Rights Fund and the other foundations that have bankrolled the Indians in their legal quest dispatch an army of well-financed lawyers to Maine to chase down other historic injustices heaped upon the Native Americans by our forefathers?," the measure passed both houses on April 3rd, after two days of debate, and was signed into law on the same day by Governor Brennan, who capitulated in his position as the chief elected opponent of the land-claim settlement by calling it "a good compromise that will make a new era in which the Indians of this state can live in dignity."

At that point, the focus of the whole land-claim case shifted to Washington, D.C., where Congress was now asked to pass a companion piece of legislation that would ratify the Maine Implementing Act, and provide eighty-one and a half million dollars to buy three hundred thousand acres of forestland for which Tureen and the members of the negotiating committee had been obtaining options for almost a year, as well as set up the twenty-seven-million-dollar trust fund that had already been agreed upon. Tureen and the negotiating committee had conditioned their willingness to recommend tribal approval of the state's jurisdictional package on the state's willingness to support this fixed-dollar settlement, as opposed to the less certain money-and-grant proposal which had been presented to the congressional delegation the previous August. By this time, however, congressional support for any settlement had become shaky, to say the least. Because of the Presidential primaries and the coming political campaign, Congress was under severe pressure to cut federal spending and achieve some semblance of a balanced budget. To make matters worse, it was precisely at this time—April of 1980—that Senator Edmund Muskie's national star began its brief ascent, with the result that, hopeful of being chosen as the Democratic nominee over a faltering President Carter, the senior senator from Maine began to cultivate his reputation as a flinty New England cost-cutter. Until then, it had appeared that Senator Muskie, who, as chairman of the Senate Budget Committee, was capable of wielding extraordinary power, would be a great asset in moving the Maine Indian Claims Settlement Act through Congress. In the spring of 1980, however, it suddenly became politically embarrassing for Muskie to champion the Indians' cause to colleagues whom he had been pressing to give up favorite measures for the sake of the Democratic Party's new emphasis upon austerity.

"We felt betrayed by Muskie," Tureen remembers. "He had been a mentor to us all along, and, following his advice, we had gone out and got Maine to agree to a settlement. Then, when we presented him with the final package in April, which was late in the congressional year, he let it sit for a critical month and a half without even calling a meeting to discuss it. And, of course, the other members of the Maine congressional delegation followed suit. So once again we began to entertain nagging doubts about the fate of the land-claims settlement. All along, you see, we had been banking on the idea that we would be able to get the support of the Carter Administration for the eighty-one and a half million dollars needed for a final settlement. However, we didn't think that Carter was going to win in November, and we knew that if we didn't get a settlement while he was still President we might very well not get one at all. In short, we realized that the joint memorandum of understanding was our personal compact with President Carter, and that it could not possibly survive his Administration. Then, just as we were beginning to entertain such gloomy thoughts in earnest, we got a couple of unexpected breaks. First of all, we were relieved of the burden of Senator Muskie's delicate political condition when, in late April, he was suddenly elevated by President Carter to the post of Secretary of State. Then, soon afterward, Governor Brennan replaced Muskie with George Mitchell, a Democrat who had run unsuccessfully against Longley five and a half years earlier, and who had been the only state politician whom the Passamaquoddies had ever endorsed. Senator Mitchell, who now inherited a seat on the Budget Committee, was perfect for the settlement for a number of reasons. To begin with, as a new senator he had few other responsibilities, and could devote his full time to the issue. Second, between 1977 and 1979 he had served as counsel of record in the Indian claim while he was United States Attorney for the District of Maine. And, most important of all, immediately prior to coming to the Senate he had been a federal judge for the United States District Court for Maine, and could thus speak with judicial authority on the legal aspects of the case, which he believed to be meritorious. In addition to having the support of Senator Mitchell, we got lucky in other areas as well. For example, as soon as Muskie got kicked upstairs Senator Cohen, who at one time supported a move to extinguish the Indian land claim, became the senior member of the Maine congressional delegation, and, recognizing that broad bipartisan support had developed in the state for a settlement, he took up the reins that Muskie had let lie, and began to move the stalled legislation forward. On June 12th, Senators Cohen and Mitchell introduced the Maine Indian Claims Settlement Act before the Senate, and scheduled hearings in the Senate Select Committee on Indian Affairs for July 1st and July 2nd."

By the time the hearings rolled around, Federal Reserve measures to combat inflation, which had been instituted earlier in the year, had begun to take hold; interest rates had plummeted; and the feeling in financial circles was that the nation was verging upon a recession. All at once, therefore, the government found itself responding to the economic necessities of the moment by designing tax cuts and planning new spending programs. This turning point could not have come at a better time for the Maine Indians, for not only was the government prepared to spend money but President Carter's campaign strategists had also apparently decided that the President had a good chance of carrying Maine in November, and they did not want to risk the President's being blamed for torpedoing a settlement that by this time had engendered the support of virtually all of the state's top political leaders.

As things turned out, the hearings on the settlement were relatively uneventful. Secretary of the Interior Cecil Andrus informed the committee that the Carter Administration would not oppose the settlement proposal, and the two members of the non-Indian opposition to the legislation, who came to the hearings to speak against the bill, had failed to get even a third of the signatures they needed to call for a referendum to suspend the Maine Implementing Act. In addition, one of them made the audience cringe by suggesting that the Indians should not be able to buy land outside their reservations because it would make non-Indian mothers uncomfortable raising their children with Indians around them. By this time, of course, much of the steam had gone out of the once vociferous and powerful opposition in Maine to the Indian land-claim settlement. Appearing before the Select Committee in support of the measure, Governor Brennan had to content himself with saying, "while I believe the State would prevail in court, I am likewise convinced that a reasonable out-of-court settlement as embodied by this legislation would better promote the interest of the people of Maine than years of bitter litigation with its inevitable adverse economic consequences"; former Governor Longley, who had planned to come to the hearings and speak in a last-ditch effort to avert the settlement, was dying of cancer at his home in Lewiston, and could not attend. As for the Indian opponents of the legislation, who described the Maine Indian Claims Settlement Act as "a sellout," they bitterly objected to the provisions and compromises that did not grant the Indians all the protections possible under federal law, and they also demanded that the Passamaquoddies and the Penobscots become a foreign nation with all the sovereign rights that such status entailed. It was a position that the members of the Select Committee on Indian Affairs were bound to react to with polite disbelief, if not bemusement, since foreign-nation status was something that the federal government was not about to recognize for any Indian tribe.

After the Senate hearings, the parties to the land-claim negotiations worked out some minor technical questions raised by the Interior Department, and on September 19th the Maine Indian Claims Settlement Act was voted out and sent to the floor of the House, where it was passed into law on September 22nd. The Senate passed the measure the following day, just before Congress recessed. When President Carter signed the act with a feather pen, on October 10th, most people in Maine felt that the long-drawn-out issue of the Indian land claim had finally been resolved.

The signing of the act by President Carter was one thing, however, and for Congress to appropriate the money to carry it out was something else, especially in the last weeks of the election campaign, when, placed on the defensive because of widespread support for Ronald Reagan's austere economic priorities, Congress had become desperately sensitive to charges that it was an irresponsibly spendthrift institution. As so often had happened in the convoluted history of the Maine Indian land claim, a last-minute hitch developed simply because, wary and defensive for reasons of their own, Tureen and the negotiating committee had demanded that the extinguishing provi-

Thomas Tureen. Photograph by Merry Farnum.

sions of the Maine Indian Claims Settlement Act, by which the Indians would forever relinquish their Nonintercourse Act claim against all of the defendants, would not go into effect until all of the eighty-one and a half million dollars was appropriated. Thanks to some arm-twisting by Senator Mitchell, however, the necessary funds were pried out of a reluctant Senate leadership, and on December 12, 1980, President Carter signed the appropriations bill for the eighty-one and a half million, which, later that day, was deposited in the Indians' account in the United States Treasury.

Since then, the two tribes have been using this money to buy land, and by the summer of 1982, they had bought a hundred and ninety thousand acres of the total of three hundred thousand acres called for in the settlement agreement. When I visited Tureen at his office in Portland, in August of that year, he told me that the Penobscots had already bought a hundred and fifty thousand acres, most of it in five large tracts. "One parcel lies east of the river," he said. "It consists of prime timberland, and it is in an area that has traditionally been a favorite Penobscot hunting and trapping ground. Another parcel, which is about twenty-five thousand acres, lies in the Carrabassett Valley, and includes most of the land surrounding the Sugarloaf Mountain Ski Area. As for the Passamaquoddies, they are proceeding in more deliberate fashion. So far, they have bought about forty thousand acres, mostly in eastern Maine. In June of 1981, they acquired a five-thousand-acre blueberry farm near Machias, in Washington County. The farm has been enormously successful during its first two seasons in Indian hands, and the tribe is now the largest independent grower of commercial wild blueberries in Maine—a particularly satisfying result considering the fact that many Passamaquoddies used to work there as pickers. Equally satisfying to the Passamaquoddies is the fact that they have reacquired four thousand of the six thousand acres in Indian Township, which were taken from them unfairly in the years that followed the signing of the 1794 treaty with Massachusetts. Incidentally, the Passamaquoddies are now negotiating with the widow of William Plaisted, who has decided to sell them the house and the tourist cabins on the shore of Lewey's Lake where the sit-in took place in 1964."

Back in February of 1980, when the newspapers were announcing that the tribes and the state were close to reaching final

agreement on the land-claim case, I spent a week among the Indians
of Maine to see how they were reacting to the news and what they
were planning for the future. My first stop was the Penobscot Reservation on Indian Island, which lies just up the Penobscot River from
the falls in Old Town, about a dozen miles north of Bangor. Indian
Island is three miles long and about a mile across at its widest point,
and at its southern end it is linked to Old Town by a single-lane steel-
girder bridge. On the day of my visit, I crossed the bridge in the early
morning; drove past St. Ann's Catholic Church, which sits near the
site of a mission established by French Jesuits in the seventeenth
century; and continued through a small, impoverished-looking community that was densely packed with single-family frame houses and
cabins, whose foundations had in many cases been wrapped with tar-
paper, plastic, or fir boughs to keep the cold out. On the far side of
the settlement, I stopped the car beside a graveyard, got out, and
spent a few minutes examining tombstones, which bore such names
as Neptune, Attien, Sapiel, Sockabesin, Lola, Francis, and Ranco.
One of the stones had an inscription that aroused my curiosity. It read,
"In memory of Louis Sockalexis, whose athletic achievements while
at Holy Cross and later with the Cleveland major league baseball team
won for him national fame."

Upon leaving the graveyard, I drove on along the road, which
soon led to a small settlement on a wooded knoll called Oak Hill.
Here, mercilessly exposed in light reflected from the ice of the frozen
river, an assortment of trailers and houses huddled together in a dreary,
snowless landscape whose brown-and-beige monotony was broken only
by the brilliantly painted hulls of overturned canoes being stored for
the winter in many of the yards. Beyond Oak Hill, the road emerged
into a huge clearing, where there was a baseball diamond with a sign
that read "Sockalexis Field"; a large, hangarlike Community Building
that contained the Penobscot Tribal Government offices; and several
smaller structures, housing a health center, a fire station, and a police
station. On the far side of the clearing, a newly paved road wound for
another mile or so through some deep woods, where, in startling
contrast to the rest of Indian Island, a modern subdivision consisting
of approximately fifty handsomely designed three-bedroom houses had
been laid out in a typical suburban pattern, employing culs-de-sac.

The subdivision marked the end of the island, and when I had
driven through it I returned to the Community Building to keep an
appointment with Andrew Akins, who was then the chairman of the

Passamaquoddy-Penobscot Negotiating Committee and tribal admin-
istrator of the Penobscot Nation. I found him in his office, at the rear
of the building, sitting beneath a framed reproduction of a proclamation that had been issued on November 3, 1755, by Spencer Phips,
lieutenant governor and commander-in-chief of the Massachusetts Bay
Colony, offering fifty pounds sterling for every male Penobscot captured and brought to Boston, twenty-five pounds for every female
prisoner, and twenty-five pounds for the scalp of an Indian child. A
goateed, strikingly handsome man now in his early forties, Akins is
Penobscot on his mother's side and Cherokee on his father's, and he
was born and raised in Old Town. After dropping out of college, in
1960, he joined the Army and was sent to Arizona, where he lived for
some years following his military service. In 1967, he enrolled in
Arizona State University, in Tempe, and upon graduating, in 1971,
he returned to Maine, where he received training in community and
economic development under a program administered by the Economic Development Administration. In 1973, using a thirty-thousand-
dollar grant from the E.D.A., Akins set up the Penobscot-Passama-
quoddy Tribal Planning Board—an organization that was given a broad
mandate by the tribes to develop and modernize the three Indian
reservations in Maine—and over the next five years he obtained some
thirty million dollars in federal funds for housing, schools, tribal-government buildings, health-care facilities, water and sewer lines, and
a public bus system, as well as for programs dealing with alcoholism,
unemployment, law enforcement, and vocational training.

"We started from scratch," he told me, in a soft voice. "There
wasn't much plumbing in some of the Passamaquoddy and Penobscot
houses, and the annual per-capita income of an Indian was only seven
hundred and fifty dollars—a third of the figure for non-Indians in
Maine. Today, all that is changed. Indian houses on the three reservations have been equipped with modern plumbing and electrical
wiring, and the average income of an Indian family has more than
doubled. Now we're going after funds to help us relearn our language.
The Passamaquoddies have had a bilingual program in their schools
for a number of years, but only a handful of Penobscots can still speak
the Penobscot language, and most of them are very old. We need to
develop a Penobscot-English dictionary, and for this we've applied for
grants from the National Endowment for the Humanities and from
the National Science Foundation that will enable us to send research-
ers to London and Paris in order to dig up the journals of early-

seventeenth-century explorers and settlers, who recorded much of our language. Imagine having to go to Europe to learn our own linguistic roots!"

When I asked Akins how he felt about the land-claim settlement that was being worked out, he smiled and shook his head. "It's far and away the most complex thing I've ever been involved in," he said. "Those of us on the negotiating committee have been working day and night for the past three weeks in an effort to iron out the final details of our future relationship with the state. Some people say that we shouldn't bother talking with the state, and that it would be better to go for broke in court. They point out that we have an airtight case, and, in the sheer legal sense, that appears to be so. However, they forget that if we did go to court it would be defendant's choice for a jury trial. Can you imagine how a jury made up of twelve white landowners would judge the merits of our claim? As for me, I can't help remembering the vileness of the reaction in Maine to the joint memorandum of understanding we negotiated with the White House. Why, it was as if we had touched a raw nerve that extended back into the innermost recesses of the true personality of the white people around here and unleashed all their deep hatred for Indians, together with their guilt for what they had done to the Indians over all the years. We had been invisible for so long, you see, that the whites simply couldn't conceive that we had any rights except those they chose to confer on us. Well, we're not invisible any longer. We're in the process of establishing our own civil and criminal laws and our own tribal courts, and once the settlement is signed and sealed we're going to take possession of our land and build upon its resources so that our children will have a better life. When that happens, we will have witnessed something that no one around here thought possible when I was young—the rebirth of an Indian nation in the state of Maine."

After leaving Akins' office, I went down the hall to chat with Glenn Starbird, a genealogist who had been working with the Penobscot Tribal Council to determine who could qualify for membership in the tribe—an increasingly important consideration now that the land-claim case was close to being settled—and with Dr. Frank Siebert, a retired pathologist, who has spent much of his life studying the Penobscot language and history. According to Starbird, who is partly of Micmac descent, probably a third of the people living in Maine today have some trace of Indian ancestry. He went on to say

Francis Ranco. Photograph by Allen Sockabasin.

that candidates for membership in the Penobscot Nation are required to prove that they are at least one-quarter Indian, of which part must be Penobscot, and that out of some fourteen hundred and fifty Penobscots who are officially recognized by the Tribal Council about four hundred and fifty live on Indian Island, an equal number live elsewhere in Maine, and the rest are scattered from California to Austria. Dr. Siebert told me that many, if not most, Penobscot and Passamaquoddy names were derivations of French names that were given to the Indians by Catholic missionaries, who converted them to Christianity and baptized them. When I asked him about some of the names I had seen on tombstones in the graveyard, he told me that Attien had come from Étienne, that Lola had been derived from Laurent, that Sapiel had originally been Xavier, and that Sockabesin had been Jacques Sébastien. When I asked about the derivation of Sockalexis, he said that the "is" at the end was an Indian diminutive, and that the name meant Jacques Little Soaring Bird.

I learned more about the Sockalexis family later in the morning, when I paid a call on Francis Ranco, who had been recommended by several of the people I talked with in the Community Building as someone who knew a good deal about the history of Indian Island. Ranco, a friendly white-haired man of seventy-nine, lives in an old house near the graveyard I had visited, and when I asked him to tell me about Louis Sockalexis he beamed with pleasure. "Louis Francis Sockalexis was one of the greatest baseball players who ever lived," he declared. "He was a hero around here when I was growing up. So was his cousin Andrew Sockalexis, who ran in the Olympic Marathon in Stockholm in 1912. But Louis was more than a hero; he was a legend. Why, people claimed he could throw a baseball clear across the river from Indian Island to the Old Town side!"

At this point, Ranco led me into his kitchen, where he rummaged through a file box, brought out an article by Bud Leavitt he had clipped from a recent edition of the Bangor *Daily News*, and handed it to me. The article described Sockalexis as a powerful hitter, a spectacular fielder, and a superb base runner, who had played baseball with extraordinary ease and grace. It went on to say that he could throw a baseball four hundred feet; that he had played at Holy Cross and Notre Dame; that between 1897 and 1899 he had been an outfielder for the Cleveland National League baseball team [the Cleveland Spiders]; that he had hit home runs in his first two times at bat at the Polo Grounds; and that following his death, in 1913, at the age of

Louis Francis Sockalexis at Holy Cross College, in 1895.
Courtesy of the Archives, College of the Holy Cross.

forty-two, the Cleveland Indians were so named in his honor. According to the newspaper story, many experts believe that Sockalexis might have become one of the greatest baseball players of all time if his career had not been abbreviated by a serious drinking problem. The account ended on a sad note. It said that Sockalexis had spent his last years drifting from one New England sandlot to another, giving batting and throwing exhibitions, which were often paid for with a drink of whiskey.

After I finished reading the article, I asked Ranco when he first became aware that the Penobscots had lost their land unfairly, and he replied that he had heard it discussed when he was a child. "The elders talked about it all the time," he said. "My father's father, Peter Ranco, told me about it when he first took me muskrat trapping, before the First World War. My other grandfather, Joseph Francis, who ran some fishing camps up on the west branch of the Penobscot River, above Millinocket, also talked about it. He told me that his great-grandfather, Sockabesin Swassin, who lived in this very house one hundred years ago, when the first nuns came to Indian Island to open up the school, had talked about it to him. During the Second World War, a cousin of mine went down to the State House in Boston and did some research on what had happened to our land. When he returned, I remember, he talked about our rights under some treaty or other, but nothing ever came of it. Then, in 1951, the bridge was built. That opened up Indian Island to visitors and new ideas. Until then, we had been awfully isolated. In the fall of the year, we often had to wait for days on end for the ice to make up thick enough to support our weight. In the late winter, we used to pack sawdust on the ice so it would last longer and we could keep driving cars across, but in the spring we would be stuck out here all over again while we waited for the ice to thaw, so we could launch our bateau ferry. It was a wooden boat that seated a dozen people, and old Sylvester Francis rowed it back and forth for years, charging ten cents a ride."

Ranco went on to say that not long after the bridge was built a lawyer from Massachusetts, whose name was Murphy, visited Indian Island and urged the Penobscots to initiate a land-claim case. "Murphy wanted us to declare our independence from Maine and then go before the United Nations and claim that we were a sovereign nation," he said. "Nothing came of that idea, because the older people, who depended on the state for relief money, were afraid that if we tried to break away from Maine they would lose everything. Murphy got us to thinking that we might have a legal case, however, and that helped pave the way for what has happened since. As for the out-of-court settlement, I predict that the people here will go for it. I know I will. Believe me, I never thought I'd live to see the day."

It was almost lunchtime when Francis Ranco and I finished talking, so I drove back to the Community Building to get something to eat at the canteen there. As I came through the front doorway, I encountered Tom Tureen, who was just coming out of the tribal governor's office. He was in the middle of what for him was a fairly typical day. He had awakened at six o'clock and breakfasted with his wife and children in the renovated farmhouse they live in, about twenty-five miles west of Portland. Then he had driven to the Portland airport, climbed into his plane, and flown to Augusta to discuss some last-minute changes in the out-of-court settlement with the state attorney general. Shortly before noon, he had flown from Augusta to a small airstrip just north of Indian Island in order to confer about the changes with the Penobscot members of the negotiating committee. He was now about to take off again and fly eastward across Washington County to Princeton, in order to spend the early part of the afternoon with his Passamaquoddy clients at the Indian Township Reservation. Then, weather and time permitting, he hoped to fly to Eastport, so that he could discuss the latest developments in the case with the Passamaquoddy leaders at the Pleasant Point Reservation. Afterward, he would fly along the coast back to Portland—a distance of some two hundred miles—climb into his car, and drive home in time to have a late supper with his wife.

Over coffee and a sandwich in the canteen, Tureen asked me to give him a lift to the airport, and said that he was eager to straighten out the final details of the settlement so that it could be ratified by the tribes, passed by the state legislature, and introduced into Congress before the summer recess. As we left Indian Island a few minutes later, he told me that he and the negotiating committee had just persuaded state officials to agree to a plan under which the three hundred thousand acres being returned to the Indians would not be subject to state property taxation. When we got to the airport, I accompanied Tureen to his plane—a blue-and-white 1972 single-engine Cessna that was parked beside a macadam runway—and he climbed in and spent a few minutes checking his instruments. Then, just before starting the engine for takeoff, he leaned through the window and gave a smile. "I'll be climbing to five thousand feet, and flying to

Princeton over some of the most beautiful forestland in the entire United States," he said. "In about fifteen minutes, I'll be looking down upon a wilderness that is going to be held in trust for the members of the Passamaquoddy and Penobscot tribes and their descendants forever."

The next day, I drove east on Route 9 from Bangor to Calais and then south on Route 1 to Perry, where I paid a brief visit to the Passamaquoddy Reservation at Pleasant Point. Pleasant Point is a small promontory that juts out from Perry into Passamaquoddy Bay, and the reservation, where some six hundred Passamaquoddies make their home, is on a treeless hundred-acre tract at its very tip. Following the 1794 treaty with Massachusetts, the Indians lived there in comparative isolation for more than a century and a half. Then, in the nineteen-fifties, without consulting the Passamaquoddies or paying for the land, the state built a causeway across the bay, linking Pleasant Point with Eastport, and proceeded to lay down a highway right through the middle of the reservation. On the day of my visit, I drove over the highway, entered the reservation, and climbed out of the car. A fiercely cold wind was blowing out of Canada across Passamaquoddy Bay, the wind-chill factor was way below zero, and the place looked and felt like an outpost in the Aleutians. I wandered around for a while, and came across a tablet mounted on a stone, which had been placed there in 1918 by the Daughters of the American Revolution. "In honor of the Indian Patriots for their loyal service during the Revolutionary War," it said. I got back in the car, drove back to Calais, and headed north on Route 1 to Indian Township, where I had an appointment to see George Stevens.

A gaunt, reticent man then in his late fifties, with sad eyes and a gentle manner, Stevens, who was director of the Housing Authority at Indian Township, as well as a member of the Passamaquoddy-Penobscot Negotiating Committee, was waiting for me in the tribal-government office building that sits by the highway, opposite Lewey's Lake. We talked a bit about the land-claim case and some of the things that had happened during the sixteen years since the day he heard the chain saw start up in the woods adjacent to his house and went outside to find out what was going on. Then we got into his car and drove out to the settlement at Peter Dana Point. On the way, Stevens showed me the house he lives in, on the shore of Lewey's Lake, where he and his wife have raised sixteen children, and the nearby tourist cabins owned by William Plaisted's widow. When we got to Peter Dana Point, he showed me the tiny cottage that Louise Sockabesin had lived in when she showed his brother John her copy of the 1794 treaty with Massachusetts, and the parish hall, where the Passama-quoddies had met when they decided to stage their sit-in. Stevens pointed out these places in a matter-of-fact way, with a minimum of elaboration, and then he turned the car around and headed back toward the tribal-government offices. Dusk was falling while we drove along Route 1. As we were approaching Stevens' house, he slowed the car, pulled it over to the side of the road, and, leaning forward, peered through the window beside me. Following his gaze, I looked across a field that lay adjacent to some woods, and saw the silhouettes of several of the Plaisted tourist cabins outlined against the frozen surface of Lewey's Lake, which was reflecting the last light of day. A few moments later, Stevens called my attention to a low mound, covered with dead grass and weeds, that sat at the edge of the field, a few yards from the car. I looked at it and then at him, and saw that he was smiling. "This is where it started," he said softly. "This is where we got arrested, and that's what's left of the sand pile."

Afterword

The claims described in this book are part of a family of lawsuits that were filed during the last two decades under the Indian Nonintercourse Act of 1790, a federal statute that outlawed the purchase or confiscation of land without the approval of Congress. For most of its existence, the Nonintercourse Act was obscure and unimportant. Title to practically all Indian land in the western part of the United States was either held in trust by the United States government (and, therefore, separately protected against alienation), or held as a result of a specific treaty that itself prohibited alienation. Since most western Indian land was taken before the creation of the western states, the federal government was normally involved in the transactions anyway. Thus, the agreements were made in conformity with the letter, if not the spirit, of the Nonintercourse Act. Many of the Indians who lived within the original thirteen states were also dealt with by the federal government. Most notable in this group were the five tribes of the southeastern United States—the Cherokee, the Creek, the Choctaw, the Chickasaw, and the Seminole—who were removed to Oklahoma by the federal government during the infamous Trail of Tears in the eighteen-thirties.

In New York State, New England, and elsewhere in the East, however, a few Indian tribes were overlooked by the federal government, generally because they were small in numbers or had been friendly to the colonists during the Revolution, and did not seem to pose a threat. Where the federal government left a vacuum, the states moved in and terminated the Indians' occupancy rights with their own treaties. Because these treaties were not approved by Congress, they violated the terms of the Nonintercourse Act, and thus gave rise to claims nearly two hundred years later.

These claims were discovered and pressed during the late nineteen-sixties and early nineteen-seventies—one of the most favorable periods for Indians in the history of the United States. Periods in which tribal lands and rights have been respected and past wrongs rectified have always been juxtaposed with periods in which Indian property, government, and values were subject to appropriation and attack. For example, from the time of the Revolution through the first two decades of the nineteenth century, the federal government treated Indian tribes as more or less equal sovereigns. During the last half of the nineteenth century, on the other hand, fully two-thirds of the total Indian land holdings in the United States were given to non-Indian settlers. The profound damage done to Indians in this period was mitigated to some extent by the Indian Reorganization Act of 1934, which encouraged tribal self-government and Indian sovereignty.

In the nineteen-fifties the pendulum swung back and Congress enacted legislation ending the special status of selected tribes. This "termination policy" was in turn officially renounced in the late nineteen-sixties, and since that time federal policy has been conducted in accordance with the Indian Self-Determination Act of 1968 and related statutes that were designed to foster tribal self-government and independence once again. While the judicial branch has been less fickle than the legislative and executive branches in its approach to Indian issues, variations in policy can nonetheless be discerned. The end of the termination era, for example, coincided with the start of a golden age of decisions from the Supreme Court concerning Indian lands, water rights, and sovereignty.

The theories underlying the claims of the Mashpee, Penobscot, and Passamaquoddy Indians were developed during the early nineteen-seventies by a group of attorneys of which I was a member. They were based upon concepts of law and questions of fact that were almost entirely untested, and they embodied many issues of first impression. Did the Nonintercourse Act apply to Indian tribes whose existence had not been recognized by the federal government? Did the Act apply in the East? What constitutes an Indian tribe for purposes of the Act? How could one prove how much aboriginal territory of a particular tribe was protected under the Act? Had the claims been erased by adverse possession or a statute of limitation? And, finally, what was the remedy for a violation of the Nonintercourse Act?

One of the most serious problems with the claims was their sheer size and the threat they posed to non-Indian interests. The claim in Maine included some twelve and a half million acres, nearly two-thirds of the state. The Mashpee claim threatened real estate development in one of the most rapidly growing resort communities in New

England. If, as all law students are taught, hard cases make bad law, these were certainly candidates for some very bad decisions. Clearly, they would press the limits of the judicial process and tempt the judges and juries who would hear them, even in the liberal nineteen-seventies, to rule with emotions rather than reason.

The two cases discussed in this book followed dramatically different courses. The litigation in Maine, which was centered on a question of law—the applicability of the Nonintercourse Act—began in an atmosphere of calm deliberation and was heard by Federal District Judge Edward T. Gignoux, a jurist who, by virtue of his national prominence and stature, was largely immune from public or political pressure. The fireworks came after he rendered the historic decision that the Act was applicable to the Maine Indians, at which point leading political figures of the state attempted to persuade Congress to eliminate the claim.

The Passamaquoddies and the Penobscots settled their claim out of court after five years of arduous negotiations for eighty-one and a half million dollars and the authority to acquire three hundred thousand acres with federal Indian territory status. Although this was far and away the largest Indian victory of its kind in the history of the United States, it was nonetheless difficult for many of the Indians to accept. For one thing, the legal issues were exceedingly complex and the risks in court hard to comprehend fully. Some of the more militant tribal members considered any resolution that did not return all the land in question and provide for absolute sovereign independence of the tribes to be a sell-out. Both militants and conservatives had a deep-seated mistrust of the federal Bureau of Indian Affairs because of the Bureau's past mismanagement and abuse of western tribes. And all Indians had been traumatized by centuries of broken treaties and bad deals at the hands of non-Indians.

The Mashpee case—a class-action lawsuit against all non-Indian landholders and the Town of Mashpee, which centered on the question of whether the Mashpees constituted a tribe for purposes of the Nonintercourse Act—resulted in fireworks in and out of the courtroom, providing front-page news for most of its forty-day trial. It was presided over by Judge Walter J. Skinner, who spent over three hours trying to set forth a definition of the term "Indian tribe," which the jury proceeded to apply against the Mashpees in a manner that can only be described as absurd.

Eleven major eastern Nonintercourse Act claims have been brought during the past fifteen years. In addition to the claims of the Mashpees and the Maine tribes, those of the Narragansett Tribe in Rhode Island and the Mashantucket Western Pequot Tribe in Connecticut have also been settled. The Narragansett Tribe, which had a claim for approximately twenty-seven hundred acres, received a little over two thousand acres in a 1978 settlement. The Pequot Tribe, which had a claim for eight hundred acres, received approximately fourteen hundred acres in a 1983 settlement.

After five years of negotiation, a settlement has finally been agreed upon in the claim of the Gay Head Indians on Martha's Vineyard, in Massachusetts. Legislation to put this settlement into effect is currently pending in both the Massachusetts legislature and the United States Congress. A settlement has also been negotiated for the claim of the Schaghticoke Tribe in Connecticut, and is awaiting introduction in the Connecticut legislature and in Congress. A settlement involving the Cayuga Tribe in New York was rejected by Congress in 1980 after the congressional representative from the area gave in to local pressure at the last minute and refused to support it. A settlement proposal put forth by the Chittamancha Tribe in Louisiana, which was introduced in 1983, was derailed by opposition from the Reagan Administration.

The claims of the Oneida and Mohawk Indians in New York, together with the Cayuga claim, involve more than six million acres and are probably the strongest of all the Nonintercourse Act claims. For these reasons, they are the most difficult to settle and are not yet the subject of serious negotiations. These claims received a substantial boost in February of 1985, when the United States Supreme Court, in a five-to-four decision, rejected arguments that ancient Nonintercourse Act claims have been barred by the passage of time. In upholding these claims, however, the Court as a whole was clearly disturbed that the law permits Indians to bring them, and pleaded with Congress to come up with a solution. Moreover, while the examples of possible congressional solutions that the Court cited were all products of negotiated settlements, the decision pointedly made no reference to negotiations with the Oneidas, thereby implying that a settlement imposed upon them by Congress might be acceptable. Still more disturbing was the final footnote in the decision, in which the Court suggested that, if the claims were litigated to the bitter end, it might ultimately hold that there is no meaningful remedy for a Nonintercourse Act violation—in other words, such a violation might not require return of land or substantial financial compensation.

The future for Indian tribes, in this writer's view, does not lie in further land claims. The Nonintercourse Act provided an opportunity for a handful of tribes in a few isolated situations to utilize the law and regain lost territory. But the situations in which the Nonintercourse Act, or other federal laws or decisions involving Indians, offers meaningful opportunities for Indians to regain lost territory and rights are extremely limited. And while the United States judicial system has displayed remarkable restraint and tolerance during the Nonintercourse Act claims, the Supreme Court has made it clear in the Oneida decision that Indians are dealing with the magnanimity of a rich and powerful nation, one that is not about to divest itself or its non-Indian citizens of large acreage in the name of its own laws. In short, the United States will permit Indians a measure of recompense through the law—indeed, it has done so to an extent far greater than any other nation in a comparable situation—but it ultimately makes the rules and arbitrates the game.

A far greater opportunity for Indian expansion and growth exists within normal commercial channels. Since their settlement, for example, the Maine Indians have pursued an aggressive investment and acquisition strategy designed to alleviate unemployment, build wealth, and create an economic presence that is changing their social and political position in the state. The Penobscots have concluded an agreement with a leading manufacturer of audio and video cassettes to build an automated cassette-manufacturing plant on their reservation at Indian Island. The Penobscots have also built an ice arena on Indian Island, which serves hockey teams from all over Maine. At the same time, the Penobscots have established a Guarantee Fund that provides financing to emerging non-Indian businesses across the state. This program not only provides a financial return to the tribe, but at the same time, and equally important, draws the Indians into the economic network from which they have been excluded for so long.

As for the Passamaquoddy Tribe, it has purchased and now operates the only cement-manufacturing plant in New England—one of the largest industrial facilities in Maine—and is the largest producer of concrete in the state. The Passamaquoddies are also the third largest producer of commercially grown wild blueberries in the world, and they own an AM-FM radio station in Rockland.

With these and similar investments, the Passamaquoddies and the Penobscots are well on their way to becoming a major financial presence in Maine. Non-Indians in the state are changing the way they view Indians, and Indians, in turn, are changing the way they view themselves. And the success of the Maine tribes is beginning to be noticed by Indian tribes in other parts of the country.

In the final analysis, the eastern Indian land claims are important because of the opportunity they afford the country as a whole to reaffirm its political, legal, and human values. Routine cases tell us little about the integrity of our system. Hard cases such as those described in *Restitution* cut to the core. The fact that people in power in the United States chose in the end to deal honorably with at least some of the eastern Indian land claims, rather than change the law to avoid an unpalatable result, is a tribute to our system. For my part, these claims provided me with the opportunity to participate in a historic, if belated, remedy for at least a few of the hundreds of Indian tribes who were displaced and disinherited by the European invasion of North America.

THOMAS N. TUREEN
April 1985